NEW ARCHITECTURE IN BRITAIN

KENNETH POWELL

NEW ARCHITECTURE IN BRITAIN

MERRELL
LONDON · NEW YORK

Published by Merrell Publishers Limited

Head office:
81 Southwark Street
London SE1 0HX

New York office:
49 West 24th Street, 8th Floor
New York, NY 10010

www.merrellpublishers.com

Publisher Hugh Merrell
Editorial Director Julian Honer
US Director Joan Brookbank
Sales and Marketing Manager Kim Cope
Sales and Marketing Executive Nora Kamprath
Managing Editor Anthea Snow
Project Editor Claire Chandler
Junior Editor Helen Miles
Art Director Nicola Bailey
Junior Designer Paul Shinn
Production Manager Michelle Draycott
Production Controller Sadie Butler

First published 2003
Paperback edition first published 2006

British Library Cataloguing-in-Publication Data:
Powell, Kenneth, 1947–
New architecture in Britain
1.Architecture – Great Britain
2.Architecture – Modern – 21st century
I.Title
720.9'41'09051

ISBN 1 85894 324 8

Designed by Maggi Smith
Edited by Sarah Yates, Kim Richardson and Kate Blake
Indexed by Laura Hicks

Printed and bound in China

ACKNOWLEDGEMENTS

My thanks go first to Hugh Merrell and Julian Honer of Merrell Publishers for commissioning this book and for their encouragement and support of the project. Emily Sanders of Merrell did a splendid job gathering in pictures and information from the sixty or so architectural practices, in Britain and abroad, that have projects included in this book. The support of those practices was obviously fundamental, and I am extremely grateful to them all and to a number of their clients for further assistance. The book has benefited from discussions with a number of friends, of whom I would particularly mention Laura Iloniemi, and Isabel Allen and Paul Finch, both of *The Architects' Journal*. I wrote about a number of the projects included here as building studies for the *AJ* and would like to dedicate this book to the British architectural press, an outstanding source of information and opinion on a subject that is increasingly recognized as critical to the social well-being and cultural vitality of Britain.

Kenneth Powell
London, 2003

Front cover and spine: Eden Project, nr St Austell, Cornwall; front cover insets (left to right): Selfridges, Birmingham (pp. 228–29), Gateshead Millennium Bridge, Gateshead, Tyne and Wear (pp. 28–29), Imperial War Museum North, Stretford, Manchester (pp. 64–65), Downland Gridshell, Weald and Downland Open Air Museum, Singleton, West Sussex (pp. 56–57), Toyota GB Headquarters, Epsom, Surrey (pp. 220–21), Baltic, Gateshead, Tyne and Wear (pp. 44–45)

Back cover: Magna Science Adventure Centre, Rotherham, South Yorkshire (pp. 110–11); back cover insets (left to right): The Deep, Kingston upon Hull, Humberside (pp. 54–55), Drop House, Firs Wood Close, Northaw, Hertfordshire (pp. 160–61), Yorkshire Sculpture Park Visitor Centre, Wakefield, West Yorkshire (pp. 88–89), VXO House, Spaniards End, Hampstead, London NW3 (pp. 192–93), Haberdashers' Hall, London EC1 (pp. 208–209)

Page 1: Darwin Centre, The Natural History Museum, South Kensington, London SW7 (pp. 52–53)

Page 2: Imperial War Museum North, Stretford, Manchester (pp. 64–65)

CONTENTS

The Willis Faber & Dumas headquarters (1975) in Ipswich, Suffolk, was a landmark in Norman Foster's career.

At the beginning of a new century, Britain can boast one of the most dynamic and fertile architectural cultures of any country in the world. London is, and has been for a decade or more, arguably the most significant centre of architectural creativity anywhere. London-based architects such as Norman Foster, Richard Rogers, Nicholas Grimshaw, Will Alsop, Zaha Hadid, Terry Farrell and David Chipperfield practise globally; for most of this group, in fact, their largest and most prestigious projects are still abroad. A decade or so ago Britain was accused of neglecting its best talents, so that Rogers and Foster, for example, achieved international fame through projects in Paris and Hong Kong respectively. Will Alsop, David Chipperfield, Nigel Coates and others had to range far afield to get jobs – Japan was one excellent source of work for a time. Practices with roots in Britain, such as Sauerbruch Hutton, Bolles & Wilson and Foreign Office Architects, continue to develop their careers outside Britain. But the charge that Britain always neglects its best talents no longer holds good. Norman Foster has come home, to change the face of London. Rogers is building a major civic monument in Birmingham, Alsop a West Midlands version of the Centre Georges Pompidou in, of all places, West Bromwich. Even Chipperfield, shamefully neglected in his own land, where the Henley Rowing Museum is his only substantial building, has a landmark commission for the BBC in Glasgow. We await Zaha Hadid's first major British building.

The architectural renaissance of the 2000s is clearly not just about London. Manchester has new buildings by Tadao Ando, Daniel Libeskind, Michael Wilford and Michael Hopkins, and a distinguished locally based school of design focused on Stephenson Bell, Ian Simpson and Stephen Hodder. The image of Tyneside is being transformed by Wilkinson Eyre's Millennium Bridge, Foster's forthcoming Sage music centre and BALTIC arts centre, Ellis Williams's striking makeover of a redundant flour mill. In Birmingham, a place many thought irredeemably ruined by the architectural and planning blunders of the 1960s, Future Systems,

Richard Rogers, Edward Cullinan, Nicholas Grimshaw and HOK are among the practices giving 'the second city' a new and more human face, while Glenn Howells and Associated Architects head up another lively local scene. Even Sheffield, with a distinctly wobbly economic base, is renewing its ravaged central area: the fiasco of Branson Coates's Pop Music Centre has been overtaken by the success of Pringle Richards Sharratt's Millennium Galleries and Winter Garden. And Liverpool, magnificent but with problems of its own, has picked the right architect, in Will Alsop, for the Fourth Grace project.

It is not just in London and the other big cities that new architecture is making its (positive) mark. It is nearly three quarters of a century since the opening of the De La Warr Pavilion put the obscure seaside resort of Bexhill-on-Sea, East Sussex, on the world architectural map. ("Bexhill has emerged from barbarism at last," wrote George Bernard Shaw.) Snøhetta & Spence's Turner Centre could do as much for Margate in Kent. (Ilfracombe in Devon, site for Tim Ronalds's Landmark Theatre, and Bridlington, East Yorkshire, where Irena Bauman and Bruce McLean's South Promenade project was completed in 1998, are other seaside resorts where new architecture seems to have made a breakthrough, and Kathryn Findlay is set to build in Hastings, East Sussex.) American superstar Frank Gehry's first British building is in Dundee, and there is the prospect of a larger project in Brighton. New York's Rafael Viñoly is working in Leicester. Britain's attachment to 'the heritage' is sometimes blamed for an alleged national failure to embrace the new and innovative. Looking at some conspicuous post-war buildings in Bath, Norwich, Cheltenham and York, one can understand why the trend for several decades was to historicist pastiche (usually extremely badly done), but the success of recent projects in those historic towns by, among others, Nicholas Grimshaw, Michael Hopkins, Feilden Clegg Bradley, Panter Hudspith and van Heyningen & Haward suggests that the tide has turned. Even the prosperous

Wilkinson Eyre's Dyson factory (1996) in Wiltshire is a striking example of modern design in a rural setting.

market town of Ludlow, Shropshire, a jewel of a place where the natural (and probably correct) reaction to developers was to suggest they looked elsewhere, has a creditable new building by Richard MacCormac (though whether Ludlow really needed Tesco remains an open question).

If 'the heritage' is a national preoccupation, 'the countryside' is an equally powerful mantra. As agriculture steadily declines, rural Britain is fought over by those who want to preserve it as a terrain for 'country sports' or turn it into a theme park or an extended housing estate, connected by new roads and serviced by out-of-town shopping and office parks. New building in the countryside has long been a contentious issue. Since the Second World War huge areas of rural land have been built over, usually with disastrous results. The defenders of the countryside, mostly drawn from the upper and professional classes, tended to be socially and culturally conservative. Traditionalist British architects such as Raymond Erith and Francis Johnson survived through the difficult years of the 1950s and 1960s, when they had little hope of public or commercial commissions, by building finely crafted houses for the rich in rural locations. In national parks and other sensitive locales, the expectation was that new buildings would be in 'traditional' style. In recent years, Michael Hopkins's David Mellor factory in the Peak District, Future Systems' house in Pembrokeshire National Park, Wilkinson Eyre's Dyson factory in Wiltshire and buildings by Feilden Clegg Bradley, Rab Bennetts and Munkenbeck & Marshall, among others, have demonstrated that high-quality modern design, on an appropriate scale, can enhance the

rural scene. Ushida Findlay's radical proposal for a new country house in Cheshire takes the traditional versus modern debate on to a new plane, invading an area of work that such architects as Quinlan Terry, Robert Adam, Julian Bicknell (and their less able emulators) have long dominated.

It is a tragic fact that most new architecture in Britain – and architects design only a small proportion of all new buildings – remains mediocre. Housing is still a black spot: there is no sign here, despite the proliferation of interesting individual houses, of the renaissance in domestic design seen, for example, in The Netherlands. Yet the British architectural scene today inspires optimism and clearly fires public interest, as the debates over buildings such as Foster's Swiss Re tower, the Scottish Parliament, Birmingham's new Selfridges and Liverpool's Fourth Grace confirm. As long ago as 1986, Deyan Sudjic celebrated the fact that architecture had been "transformed from an intensely private debate, carried out on paper and in the smoke-filled rooms of architectural schools, into a matter of genuine public concern, fought out on the streets once more".[1] Today the debate remains as intense as ever, reflecting the way in which the art of architecture impacts on every aspect of human life and, in one of the most densely populated countries in the world, can enrich lives – or wreck them.

Fifty years ago, architecture was certainly seen as such a private debate. The pre-war Modern Movement had been, by and large, a gentleman's pursuit, with the construction of one-off residences for the artistically minded rich as its principal preoccupation. Its proponents would not, of course, have seen it in that light. The MARS (Modern Architecture Research) Group, founded in 1934, with Wells Coates as first chairman, was committed to social progress. After 1945 modern architects were given the chance to change the face of Britain. Private houses were laid aside in favour of mass housing, schools, hospitals and factories. Architects such as Edward Cullinan, Jeremy Dixon and Richard Rogers, all of whom studied at the Architectural Association school in the 1950s, recall the fervour with which the social gospel was proclaimed. The commercial field, which was rapidly coming to life again, was dismissed as an immoral diversion; few 'serious' architects – perhaps Gollins Melvin Ward was an exception – designed office blocks. Commercially minded architects such as Richard Seifert and Fitzroy Robinson, who did not share these scruples, were able to found large and lucrative practices working exclusively for the private developer sector.

The distinction between 'good' and 'commercial' architecture persisted into the 1980s and still resonates today. As early as 1959 John Summerson had argued that the idea of architecture as an ideological 'cause' was now a distraction at best. "It is architecture or nothing," he wrote. "And if it is architecture, it is architecture continually redefined – not in words but in forms."[2] In 1959, in fact,

the post-war reconstruction programme had yet to reach its zenith. A few years later, the Labour Party was calling for 500,000 new houses to be built annually; the Tory government promised 400,000. The construction industry's response to the challenge included the development of system-building techniques. High-rise developments, which actually accounted for only a quarter of all new housing built between 1945 and 1969, provided post-war cities with a new image.[3] The Ronan Point disaster of 1968, when a tower block in Newham, London, collapsed, effectively marked the end of the high-rise construction programme.

Young architects trained after the Second World War were usually encouraged to think of Le Corbusier as a near god, but by the early 1970s his crown had slipped. Jane Jacobs's *The Death and Life of Great American Cities* (1961), an anti-clearance polemic, began to be widely read, and its lessons applied to Britain. Community campaigners allied with conservationists to fight surviving clearance proposals. The conservation lobby was well established – William Morris had launched the Society for the Protection of Ancient Buildings in 1877 – but it now acquired a new fervour. SAVE Britain's Heritage was founded in 1975 (European Architectural Heritage Year) to fight for everything from Palladian mansions to jute mills. In the same year John Betjeman,

Hunstanton School (1949–54), Hunstanton, Norfolk, by Peter and Alison Smithson, was a landmark of the New Brutalism.

The Halifax Building Society headquarters (completed in 1975) in Halifax, West Yorkshire, by Building Design Partnership (BDP), is a vigorously modern response to the context of a Victorian industrial town.

poet and preservationist, condemned redevelopment as a cynical exercise – "the swish perspective tricked up by the architect's firm to dazzle the local councillors".[4] Architects got their comeuppance, some felt, with the economic collapse that followed the energy crisis of 1973. Jobs dried up and newly qualified architects struggled to find employment.

The certainties of the old Modern Movement had, in fact, come under fire back in the 1950s from the revisionists of Team X. The so-called New Brutalism, with which Peter and Alison Smithson and Stirling & Gowan were associated, was a revolt against the smooth uniformity of the International Style by young architects who found much to admire in East End streets and High Victorian Gothic. Unfortunately, the usual response of architects to public disillusionment with Modernism was less rigorous. 'Neo-vernacular' was a broad term for an architecture that simply threw in the sponge and opted for inoffensive brick cladding and pitched roofs. Its practitioners could draw on some recent precedents: Edward Cullinan, for example, had put a stone-slate pitched roof on his Minster Lovell study centre, in Oxfordshire, in the 1960s. Cullinan was seeking an alternative programme of modern design – the quest continues to generate outstanding work by his practice – but many of his imitators, sadly, were mere style mongers. The *Architectural Review*

described Cullinan and MacCormac as "Romantic Pragmatists" (a term neither much liked), hinting at their roots in the Arts and Crafts Movement and the American school of Wright, Maybeck and others. Cullinan or MacCormac would have rejected even more sharply the label 'Post-modernist'.

The mainline Modernist tradition persisted through the difficult years of the 1970s in the work, for example, of Ahrends, Burton & Koralek (ABK, one of the most consistently interesting practices on the British scene), Powell & Moya, Howell Killick Partridge Amis and others. One of the best provincial buildings of the 1970s was the massive headquarters for the Halifax Building Society in Halifax, West Yorkshire, by Building Design Partnership (BDP), firmly inspired by American HQ models. In London, the Barbican arts centre, the last element in Chamberlin, Powell & Bon's monumental Barbican project, opened only in 1982. Denys Lasdun, who had practised before the war with Berthold Lubetkin, worked on into the 1990s, although his National Theatre, London, was to become the last monument of the heroic Modern tradition in Britain. Lasdun regarded Post-modernism as morally, as well as aesthetically, offensive. But the Post-modern tide, American-inspired, swept over such commercial practices as Fitzroy

Denys Lasdun's National Theatre (1969–76) on London's South Bank: a controversial but heroic Modern Movement monument.

Robinson, Chapman Taylor, Seifert, BDP and even Yorke, Rosenberg & Mardall (YRM – once a bastion of the Modern Movement) just as the development boom of the Thatcher era was providing them with plenty of commissions. (Seifert's crude office scheme along Farringdon Road in London was one of the worst of a bad bunch, a tragedy for a firm that had once produced the style icon of Centre Point in the capital.) Modern architecture, Charles Jencks proclaimed, was dead. Instead of functionalism and social engineering, architecture should be about communication: "An architect's primary and final role is to express the meanings a culture finds significant," Jencks wrote.[5]

Post-modernism was not just about style or 'meaning', but also about the relationship of buildings to the city. The street had to be rediscovered: Jeremy Dixon's St Mark's Road housing in North Kensington, London, was a pioneering exercise in this process, begun in 1975, while the office of Campbell, Zogolovitch, Wilkinson & Gough (CZWG) sold streetwise housing to the commercial sector with its early projects for Kentish Homes. (CZWG's Piers Gough became a well-known public figure and remains a wise and witty commentator on the present-day scene.) During the 1970s James Stirling, who was building virtually nothing, began to explore historical sources for inspiration. His new

Classical preoccupations found supreme expression in the Staatsgalerie Stuttgart, opened in 1983. For all his global fame, Stirling (who died tragically early in 1992) built relatively little in Britain after 1970. The most prominent Post-modernist landmarks in London were the work of Terry Farrell, whose long and productive partnership with Nicholas Grimshaw terminated in 1980. Partly trained in the USA, Farrell was greatly influenced by the urbanistic polemics of Robert Venturi, Colin Rowe and Fred Koetter.[6] Although best known for monumental new buildings such as Vauxhall Cross (the headquarters of the intelligence agency MI6) and the Charing Cross station redevelopment, both in London, Farrell displayed particular expertise at urban reconstruction and the conversion of old buildings. The Comyn Ching Triangle (Covent Garden) and TV-AM projects, the latter now much altered, remain among his best. Outside London, Farrell established a base in Edinburgh, where the prominent convention centre was his largest work and the Dean Gallery (a magical makeover of a Victorian orphanage) undoubtedly his best. Farrell's response to the recession of the early 1990s was to transfer operations to the Far East, where he built on a large scale (notably the huge Inchon airport in Seoul). Focusing again on Britain, Farrell designed a headquarters building for Samsung in west London; the project was a

victim of recession in the Far East but could have been one of the truly spectacular office buildings of the late twentieth century. Heritage Lottery schemes in Newcastle upon Tyne (the Centre for Life) and Hull (The Deep) kept the Farrell office busy, and by 2003 Farrell was working on projects across Britain, including the new Home Office in Marsham Street, Westminster, a large London Docklands development for Rupert Murdoch's News International and a masterplan for the Greenwich Peninsula. Farrell is sometimes accused of inconsistency, of perennially looking for new stylistic devices, a charge he dismisses. For Farrell, populism is nothing to be ashamed of but purism is a dead end: he seeks to design in tune with a place. The Deep, for example, sometimes seen as inspired by the work of Daniel Libeskind and Frank Gehry, is, says Farrell, a product of its site, engineered like a ship and rising out of the strata of the Humber estuary.

If one British practice seems to have inherited the Stirling mantle, however, it is not Terry Farrell's but the partnership of Jeremy Dixon and Edward Jones, formed in 1989 (although Dixon and Jones had collaborated since their time at the Architectural Association). The Royal Opera House project in London's Covent Garden, on which Dixon began work in 1984, was a heroic operation – completing it fifteen years later won Dixon a knighthood – and a prime example of urban repair. The reconstruction of the Covent Garden piazza elevations is a true Post-modern triumph, the rest of the scheme a rather mixed bag. (The idea of an accessible and permeable public complex has not been realized.) Dixon.Jones's work is, on occasions, surprisingly formal – the Said Business School in Oxford is a prime example – but the practice is equally able to respond boldly to complex urban and spatial dilemmas. The Henry Moore Centre in Leeds, one of the few interesting recent buildings in this dynamic but architecturally timid city, is a superb urban gesture, both marking and healing a gash in the townscape. The Ondaatje Wing at London's National Portrait Gallery (NPG) is perhaps Dixon.Jones's finest work to date, creating a lot of useful space out of a forgotten backland and completing the NPG's transformation into a front-rank national museum. Not surprisingly, Charles Saumarez Smith, Dixon.Jones's client at the NPG, has taken the practice with him to the National Gallery, London, where a major revamp is planned in response to Norman Foster's reconfiguration of Trafalgar Square.

Foster, peer and member of the Order of Merit, remained the dominant figure in British architecture at the beginning of the twenty-first century. The Hongkong and Shanghai Bank

Centre Point (1961–66), New Oxford Street, London: contentious when built, Seifert's office tower has become a popular landmark in the capital and is now a listed building.

made him a global figure but he had already completed an equally significant work in the superb Willis Faber & Dumas headquarters (1975) in Ipswich, Suffolk. The new airport terminal at Stansted, opened in 1991, reflected Foster's renewed grip on the British scene. Since then he has been unstoppable: the British Museum Great Court, Millennium Bridge, City Hall and Swiss Re tower are among the prime sights of contemporary London, and the new Wembley Stadium is well on its way. The scale of Foster's operation is, by British standards, remarkable in itself – a total payroll of nearly 600 – and a constant supply of work is needed to keep it employed. These include projects that might, by Foster's standards, appear unexceptional. Foster has himself said that innovation comes from bespoke buildings, designed with an end-user in mind. There is little obviously radical about the various recent City buildings (Swiss Re excluded) designed by the Foster office, nor about the HSBC tower at Canary Wharf or the office buildings at London Bridge City. Yet each of them has a distinctive quality: in the field of spec offices, where Foster leads, others follow. The example was set in the 1980s by Stuart

Lipton and other progressive developers, who argued that cheapness and good value are not the same thing.

Foster's former partner and fellow peer, Richard Rogers, who celebrated his seventieth birthday in 2003, has also moved decisively into the commercial field, with one of the best recent spec office buildings in Britain at Wood Street in the City, an entire office park at Chiswick, west London, and other big commercial projects in the pipeline, alongside such major international commissions as Madrid airport and the Antwerp law courts. There was a time when both Foster and Rogers were bracketed together as High-tech architects – although each had a distinctive approach to design – when they emerged amid the general gloom of the 1970s. Recent projects by the two offices, however, reflect increasingly divergent strategies. Although Foster has opted more and more for strong, non-orthogonal, even 'organic', forms, his buildings remain smooth and contained structures in the tradition of Mies van der Rohe, while those of Rogers, ever anxious to articulate the circulation of people and services, still retain something of the expressive 'Gothic' quality that many detected in the iconic Lloyd's of London. Such recent

Dixon.Jones's reconstruction and extension of the National Portrait Gallery (1994–2000), London, utilized backland space to create striking light-filled galleries.

The terminal building at Stansted Airport, completed in 1991, was one of Norman Foster's first major works in Britain after the completion of the Hongkong and Shanghai Bank in 1986.

projects as the Bordeaux law courts and Lloyd's Register of Shipping, London, reflect the influence of Rogers's younger design partners, Ivan Harbour and Graham Stirk. The urban agenda of the office is never far below the surface. Although Rogers suffered from the media campaign against the Millennium Dome, his positive role in launching the regeneration of the whole Greenwich Peninsula was conveniently overlooked.

High-tech (a critics' label that none of its alleged practitioners ever liked) was the salvation of British architecture after the collapse of old-style Modernism. The work of Nicholas Grimshaw retains an explicit preoccupation with structure and an almost obsessive concern for detail – his steel castings are famous – which suggests a predominantly technological agenda. In fact, Grimshaw's recent work defies easy categorization. His Frankfurt Messehalle (2000) contains what is claimed as the largest column-free space in Europe. The Eden Project in Cornwall is one of the most successful Lottery projects and a huge popular success. The proposed Minerva Tower could be one of London's best tall buildings. In addition, Grimshaw is set to reconstruct Paddington station, convert Battersea Power Station as a vast leisure facility and construct a major extension to the Royal College of Art (all in London) while extending his operations in the USA.

Michael Hopkins formed an independent practice, with his wife, Patty, in 1976 after an eight-year partnership with Norman Foster. His early work was firmly within the High-tech enclosure. During the later 1980s Hopkins looked increasingly

to a wide range of historical sources and began using a variety of 'traditional' materials, such as timber, lead, brick and stone, and jettisoning lightness and indeterminacy for weight and permanence. The Mound Stand at Lord's Cricket Ground, London, the opera house at Glyndebourne, East Sussex, the David Mellor factory in Derbyshire and the reconstruction of Albert Richardson's Bracken House, London (England's first post-war listed building), demonstrated Hopkins's ability to work with context and history. Among his recent work, Haberdashers' Hall, London, is firmly within the crafted contextual mould, while the extension to Manchester City Art Gallery has a cool and elegant rigour reflecting the influence of Louis Kahn. Hopkins has not built outside Britain.

The Foster and Rogers studios generated a number of the new practices of the 1980s and 1990s, including the now-dissolved partnership of Jamie Troughton and John McAslan, Stanton Williams, Lifschutz Davidson, Marks Barfield, Wilkinson Eyre (winners of the Stirling Prize in 2001 and 2002) and Ian Ritchie Architects. Czech-born Jan Kaplicky, who spent periods in the offices of both Rogers and Foster, formed Future Systems as an experimental think-tank. Kaplicky's ideas, which restated the ideals of impermanence and flexibility, were dismissed as impractical for many years. Although the practice narrowly failed to win the competition for Paris's Bibliothèque nationale de France in 1989, the completion of the media centre at Lord's Cricket Ground (1999), fabricated like a ship, and the commission for a new Selfridges store in Birmingham (opened in 2003) saw Kaplicky's ideas translated into buildings.

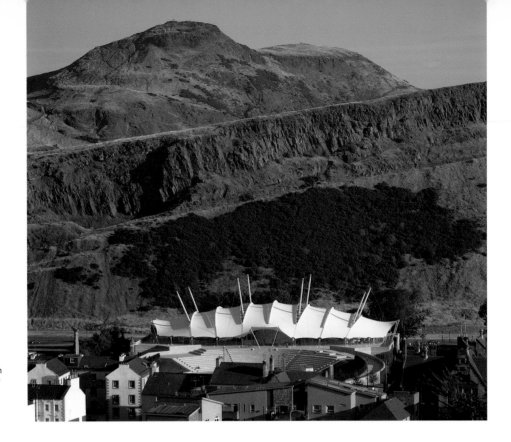

The William Younger Centre – Dynamic Earth in Edinburgh features the masted-fabric roof that became something of a hallmark of Michael Hopkins's architecture during the 1990s.

The renaissance of form in architecture is hardly a British phenomenon: internationally it is reflected in the work of Gehry, Rem Koolhaas, Libeskind and others, and is evident in that of Foster, Rogers and Farrell. Will Alsop, born in 1947, is of a younger generation than the last three. As a young architect he worked for Cedric Price, a maverick figure whose concern for flexibility and portability (which paralleled that of the Archigram group) and equally significant pursuit of social relevance made a strong impression on Alsop (although the latter has never shared Price's marked anti-aesthetic bent). After flirting briefly with Post-modernism, however, Alsop developed his own manner during the 1980s. Eschewing the High-tech interest in structure and services, Alsop starts his projects as sketches and paintings, working them into designs for buildings in collaboration with his multi-disciplinary office team and with the client. Alsop's first major built scheme was the Hôtel du Département in Marseilles, won in competition in 1990. In recent years, he has completed the Stirling Prize-winning library in Peckham, south London, with its reading room raised on legs high above the inner-city streets, and the sensuous and colourful Jubilee line extension station at North Greenwich, next to the Rogers Dome. While working extensively abroad, Alsop is also building around Britain, working on several office schemes, a medical school, university buildings and a community centre in London, a masterplan for Barnsley, a major regeneration project for Urban Splash in east Manchester, the reconstruction of New Street station in Birmingham, and the Fourth Grace in Liverpool – not to mention the c/PLEX

project in West Bromwich, now on site and a reminder that Alsop, when not yet qualified as an architect and working with Archigram-veteran Dennis Crompton, managed to come second in the 1971 Pompidou Centre competition. Alsop's position in the very front rank of contemporary British architects now looks assured, after years when he was widely seen as a marginal, even extreme, figure. He has won through not by compromising but by sticking to his guns.

London's role as an international architectural capital is reflected in the presence there of Zaha Hadid, an architect of real genius who has yet to realize a project in Britain, although she is now building on a considerable scale across the world. (Her first British building will be a cancer care centre in Scotland.) The cancellation of Hadid's opera house at Cardiff Bay robbed Wales of a building to rival Gehry's Guggenheim Bilbao and even the Sydney Opera House as an innovative landmark. It is also in London that Britain's two leading architecture schools, the Architectural Association and the Bartlett, are located, which are remarkable not only for training architects but also as fertile sources of new thinking about the art of architecture.

The failure of British Modernism to generate a culture of architecture and design helps to explain the success of the Prince of Wales's much-publicized architectural campaigns, launched in 1984. The prince was able to capitalize on the continuing public resentment against modern architecture, which was an unexpected by-product of the post-war reconstruction programme. Having championed 'community architecture', he became increasingly preoccupied by stylistic issues and was much influenced by the visionary architect–planner Leon Krier. The prince was accused, not unfairly, of being a negative critic, with nothing constructive to contribute to the architectural debate and a tendency to pick on good architects and leave the mediocre unscathed. (His outspoken attack on the well-respected ABK, which lost them the National Gallery extension, was particularly resented by the profession.) His response, in 1989, was to commission Krier to plan a major extension on Duchy of Cornwall land to the town of Dorchester, Dorset – the Poundbury Farm development, which would double the population of the place. The new 'quarters' would be planned on traditional lines, with low-rise housing to a relatively high density, streets and squares, and appropriate public buildings, including places of worship, pubs and market halls and a degree of 'clean' industry. (Krier argued that zoning had destroyed the life of towns.) The 1990s recession slowed the rate of development at Poundbury but within a decade there was enough built to judge the success of the scheme. The housing had proved highly saleable but the population was overwhelmingly middle class, with a high proportion of retirees – none of the mix of classes that the prince had admired in Italian hill towns. The most prominent public building was a market hall designed by John Simpson, apparently based on the hall at Tetbury, Gloucestershire, the nearest town to the prince's Highgrove estate. Compared with most new housing development in the countryside, Poundbury has much to offer, yet so far (and development continues) it seems a sterile place, simply too earnest, too well groomed and rather precious, with nothing of the life of 'real' towns.

John Simpson (born 1954) came to prominence as a result of the prince's campaigning activities (which were later redirected towards the field of education and regeneration). In 1988 the young Classicist produced alternative proposals for developing Paternoster Square in London, the area of 1960s offices to the north of St Paul's Cathedral for which Arup Associates had produced redevelopment proposals. Backed by the prince, Simpson's masterplan (with a substantial input from Terry Farrell) of streets, squares and traditional City blocks was eventually taken up by the site owners and won planning consent. It was, however, a victim of the 1990s recession. Simpson's proposals for London Bridge City, Phase II – 'Venice on the Thames' – were also abandoned, and the site is now being filled with buildings by Foster and Partners.

When Simpson's Queen's Gallery at Buckingham Palace, with strong undertones of Sir John Soane and John Nash, opened in 2002 it received a generally favourable press from critics; if they did not actually love it, they were happy to regard it as, at worst, a harmless (and well-crafted) oddity. The threat apparently posed by the New Classicism around 1990 had receded and Simpson, Quinlan Terry (Erith's successor) and other Classicists were safely corralled doing country houses and a handful of buildings at Oxford and Cambridge universities. Terry, a senior figure (born 1937 and based in rural East Anglia) who had never sought an alliance with the prince, completed the last of his six villas at Regent's Park, London, in 2003. Robert Adam (who works from Winchester) and Demetri Porphyrios, however, remain active in the commercial field: Porphyrios has completed office buildings in Birmingham and Reading and is working with Allies & Morrison on the masterplan for King's Cross, London. Yet the days when Classicists would routinely be included on shortlists for major public projects have gone. And there seems to be a marked absence of new talent in the traditionalist camp. One of the most lively historicist schemes of recent years, Richard Griffiths's Millennium Project at Southwark Cathedral, is Gothic rather than Classical in inspiration, while there is clearly a genuine feeling for tradition in the work of Cullinan, MacCormac and others who would hate to be seen as anything but modern architects. Cullinan's post-fire reconstruction of St Mary's Church, Barnes, south-west London, in the mid-1980s was a marker for 'new/ old' projects, but the field of conservation architecture in Britain has been largely characterized by a preservationist imperative. Only recently has the dynamic juxtaposition of the historic with the new, pioneered in Italy, for example, by Scarpa, Albini and BBPR from the 1950s on, become familiar in Britain via projects by Stanton Williams, Richard Murphy and others. Levitt Bernstein's rebuilding of the derelict shell of St Luke's Church, Old Street, London, completed in 2003, is a particularly bold expression of this approach.

If the architectural battle ten years ago seemed to be between High-tech and Classicism, today it is the advocates of expressive free form who are pitted against a more conservative and rational modern tradition. Leslie Martin (1908–2000) achieved fame for his work on the Royal Festival Hall, London (always a genuinely popular building and one that is again influencing contemporary design), and subsequently as chief architect to the London County Council. As head of the architecture department at Cambridge University (1956–72) Martin generated a school of design. Colin St John Wilson, Martin's acolyte and sometime professional collaborator, took over London's

British Library project from his master in the 1960s and, heroically, saw it through to completion thirty years later. Although thoroughly out of step with contemporary architectural fashion by the time of its completion and ill-adapted to its gritty site, the library is a finely crafted building and an expression of the 'alternative' modern tradition that Wilson champions, with a strong dose of Alvar Aalto among its inspirations. Barry Gasson, also a product of the Cambridge school, was responsible for another cultural monument in which Scandinavian influences are detectable, Glasgow's Burrell Collection (opened 1983); the building proved hugely popular but Gasson has built little since. David Lea, another Cambridge alumnus, was responsible for a residential building at the Royal Agricultural College in Cirencester praised by the Prince of Wales, among others, although its interpretation of the Cotswold tradition was far from literal. Lea's recent work has been small-scale and concentrated in north Wales, where he lives. Eric Parry, although not trained at Cambridge, has taught at the school for many years (along with such figures such Peter Carolin and Dalibor Vesely) and was even responsible for recasting the interior of its building. Bob Allies, a partner since 1984 in the phenomenally successful practice of Allies & Morrison,

is another former teacher there. With his Cambridge-trained partner, Graham Morrison, Allies has generated a version of the 'alternative' tradition that focuses on fastidious detail, fine materials, a concern for context and history and a tendency to understatement and good manners; this again draws on Scandinavian precedents as well as the English Arts and Crafts Movement. Andrew Saint found their work "reflective;"[7] others have found it dull, but its rationalism, Martinesque emphasis on quality and *utilitas* and adaptability to a wide range of locales help to explain the continuing rise of the practice. Allies & Morrison's work is certainly English to the core: it does not seem to export.

The idea of architecture as social service, dear to the Modern Movement, has received a boost in recent years after the trough of the Thatcher era, with renewed investment in 'social' housing, schools and hospitals. On the school front, Hampshire County Council's chief architect, Colin Stansfield-Smith, led a building campaign that bucked the trend and continued through the 1980s, involving architects such as Cullinan and Hopkins as well as a strong in-house team. Indeed, the programme continues: the Whiteley primary school at Fareham (project architect: Nev Churcher) won a Royal Institute of British Architects (RIBA) award in

Barry Gasson's Burrell Collection gallery in Glasgow is a sensitive response to the green setting of Pollok Park. Uncompromisingly modern, the museum was hugely popular from the time of its opening in 1983.

2002. Practices such as Phippen Randall Parkes, Hunt Thompson, Levitt Bernstein, Pollard Thomas Edwards and Avanti Architects continued to build social architecture of solid quality through some lean years. The involvement of many new practices in this field, however, is refreshing. At the old-established, but remarkably dynamic, Peabody Trust (which owns 20,000 homes in London) Dickon Robinson has proved an enlightened and bold client, not content to opt for the safe and the familiar. Cartwright Pickard's prefabricated Murray Grove housing in Hackney, London, built in twenty-seven weeks in 1998–99, was an experiment that paid off. Bill Dunster and Allford Hall Monaghan Morris are among other practices that have worked for Peabody. On the South Bank, London, Coin Street Community Builders has created a lively and stylish new residential quarter working with Lifschutz Davidson and Haworth Tompkins. The Millennium Village at Greenwich looks promising, with a mix of public and private housing by Ralph Erskine and Proctor Matthews and a school/social centre by Cullinan. Outside London, the Joseph Rowntree Foundation has built outstanding CASPAR developments (rented accommodation for young professionals) in Birmingham and Leeds (by Allford Hall Monaghan Morris and Levitt Bernstein respectively).

Public housing long enjoyed the reputation as a last resort. Now largely freed from the monopoly power of local authorities and more responsive to the needs of residents, it is setting a standard that the private sector aspires to. North-west-based Urban Splash, founded by Tom Bloxam and Jonathan Falkingham, pioneered the conversion of historic buildings in Liverpool and Manchester, often former mills and warehouses, into high-quality housing. In Liverpool, for example, it rescued the 1840s Collegiate School, a magnificent Tudor Revival structure, from total ruin with a new apartment building slotted behind the preserved façades by Falkingham's Shed KM practice. Smithfield Buildings in Manchester, with Stephenson Bell as architect, effectively launched the 'loft revolution' in the city. Urban Splash's new-build projects involve leading architects such as Glenn Howells (Timber Wharf in Manchester) and Will Alsop (New Islington in east Manchester, a true urban village with 1400 homes, shops, schools, health centre and sports facilities). As the large quantity of new speculative housing in London and the centres of Birmingham, Manchester, Leeds and Newcastle confirms, private buyers in urban areas want a modern aesthetic as well as modern comforts. The traditional 'volume' developers, of which Berkeley Homes is the largest, have been unadventurous in their choice of

architects, to say the least. But maybe this will change: St George, for example, a subsidiary of Berkeley, commissioned Patel Taylor for its Putney Bridge project, a striking makeover of a dumb 1960s office slab, while Berkeley itself went to Ian Ritchie for its high-rise Potters Field development in Southwark (both London). Even conservative Cheltenham, where until recently it was hard to build in any style but mock-Georgian, has the excellent Century Court housing by Feilden Clegg Bradley (who are also responsible for the high-style Point scheme in Bristol).

Many of these projects reflect the agenda of the Urban Task Force report that Richard Rogers's committee delivered to the Blair government in 1999. The regeneration bandwagon had, in fact, begun to roll in the Thatcher era. Mrs Thatcher's free-market agenda was balanced by the interventionist policies of the environment secretary Michael Heseltine, who established development corporations in London Docklands and other major conurbations with a brief to secure investment and development using public money as a catalyst to attract private-sector interest. Although politically contentious – the corporations, with full planning powers, bypassed local authorities, most of which were 'old' Labour run – Heseltine's initiative secured results. New-style developers such as Harry Handelsman of the Manhattan Loft Corporation began to look at derelict industrial buildings and to see their potential for stylish conversion. A number of pioneering projects, including some by Urban Splash, depended on underwriting from public funds. The torch of regeneration has been taken up outside London by the new regional development agencies such as Advantage West Midlands and Yorkshire Forward (the latter is the client for Will Alsop's projected 'Tuscan hill town' transformation of Barnsley). The regeneration programme and the continued boom in public building is underpinned by the largesse of the Treasury. In July 2002 Chancellor Gordon Brown committed £30 billion for spending on such projects, which was predicted by *Building Design* to produce "an avalanche of new construction work".[8] With such sure foundations, the construction industry and the architectural profession looked well equipped to ride out any recessionary tremors in the private sector.

The problem is that many, including Richard Rogers, have expressed doubts as to whether the largesse is being spent in the right way. The Task Force called for the reclamation of 'brownfield' urban land for housing and the densification of cities, yet housing development continues

The Queen Elizabeth II Great Court (1994–2003) at the British Museum, London, by Foster and Partners is a spectacular public space in what was previously a dank courtyard filled with book stacks.

to sprawl into the countryside, often at very low densities. Rick Mather's 1900-unit housing development, on a 12.5-hectare (31-acre) site close to the station in Milton Keynes (a new town of the 1960s with all too obvious space for greater density) is clearly the way forward. Allowing just eleven houses to be built on a 3.5-hectare (8.5-acre) site on the edge of the Worcestershire village of Tutnall is a disgrace: the planning system must bolster the regeneration process. The government's capitulation to the roads lobby and the effective collapse of its public transport policy weakened the case for dense urban development and opened up the path to further incursions into the countryside. The transport secretary John Prescott's proposals in 2003 for 200,000 new homes in the Thames corridor, east of London, seemed to open the way for more low-rise sprawl.

Richard Rogers was founding chairman of the Architecture Foundation, and his role as an adviser to the government might seem a hopeful sign. The Blair administration's establishment of the Commission for Architecture and the Built Environment (CABE) as the replacement for the Royal Fine Art Commission was equally positive. In 2001 Prime Minister Tony Blair put his name to the Better Public Building Award, with the aim of proving that good design is not a costly luxury. The first prize went to Tate Modern in London. Yet many government policies, or at least the way in which they are applied, seem to undermine the drive for design quality. The Private Finance Initiative (PFI) is the prime example. "How did we dream up a system where a single PFI provider can use a single, undistinguished architect to design 35 schools in one area?" asked Will Alsop, Rogers's successor at the Architecture

Foundation.[9] Early in 2003 the Audit Commission concluded that PFI-built schools were "considerably poorer" than those procured by traditional methods. CABE's growing involvement with PFI projects is intended to raise the quality threshold, and in Hampshire schools continue to be built without PFI, drawing on funds accumulated through land sales, and the high standards set by Colin Stansfield-Smith are being maintained. For most public projects, however, PFI rules and the results are often dire. The refurbished Treasury building in Whitehall (a Foster and Partners project) was claimed as a PFI success story, as was Anshen Dyer's £230,000,000 Norfolk & Norwich Hospital, certainly a striking building but with fewer beds than the old hospital it replaced. The debate continues. New Labour's pro-privatization obsession fuelled its potentially disastrous treatment of the London Underground, while the extraordinary achievement of the Jubilee line extension was rubbished. In fact, this project set an exemplary standard for renewing the infrastructure.

In one sense, well-managed PFI could be seen as a means of keeping architects involved in projects that might otherwise join the great majority of construction jobs in which architects have no part. The pressure from the construction industry, and even from the RIBA, on architects to reform their ways of working in tune with the 'real' world could be read in the same light. 'Design and build' is now an established way of getting buildings built, yet it diminishes the role of the architect and the results can be disastrous. Perhaps it is partly in response to these pressures that the status of architecture as an art is being reaffirmed.

There is no sign of public interest in architecture diminishing. The major projects funded by the Millennium

Commission and other Lottery bodies started to dry up after 2000 but a number were considerable popular successes – Grimshaw's Eden Project in Cornwall, Wilford's The Lowry in Salford, Farrell's The Deep in Kingston upon Hull, Libeskind's Imperial War Museum North in Manchester and Wilkinson Eyre's Magna Science Adventure Centre in Rotherham, along with London schemes such as the British Museum Great Court and Tate Modern. (Others, such as the Pop Music Centre, Sheffield, the Earth Centre, Doncaster, and Millennium Point in Birmingham, folded or struggled to survive.) These projects undoubtedly generated new interest in architecture. In 2003 there is a growing willingness among the public to accept radical work that a decade or so ago would have raised storms of protest.

The gulf between London and the regions remains, of course. Commercial development beyond London is still dominated by large regional practices, many of them with no aspirations to design excellence or innovation. Yet the auguries are good. In Leeds, a booming city with hardly any recent building worth a second glance, Buschow Henley and Allford Hall Monaghan Morris are at work. The recent record of Manchester, Gateshead, Walsall and Wakefield is hugely encouraging. The new Scotland, now with its own parliament, might be expected to shine. The Glasgow Year of Architecture in 1999 produced some built spin-offs, Page & Park's Lighthouse and the Homes for the Future project, but the spirit it generated seems largely to have evaporated. Despite the excellent work done by Richard Murphy, Malcolm Fraser, McKeown Alexander and Nicoll Russell, there are few signs of Scotland developing a distinctive school of its own – and too many of a retreat into a bogus 'Scottishness' (a vice of which Page & Park's visitor attraction at Loch Lomond has been widely accused). Wales lacks the home-grown talents of Scotland and has been unreceptive to those of distinguished outsiders. The saga of the Welsh Assembly building is the latest chapter in a story of missed opportunities – will the Assembly do the right thing, admit it got it wrong and reappoint Richard Rogers? Perhaps the launch of a Welsh version of CABE will begin the re-education of the principality.

The future of architecture, in Britain and elsewhere, is linked to such vital issues – the fate of our cities, the housing crisis and the protection of the world's fragile environment – that discussion of style seems almost irrelevant. Practices such as Edward Cullinan Architects, Bennetts Associates, Feilden Clegg Bradley, Bill Dunster (architect of the groundbreaking BedZED project in Beddington, Sutton) and Cottrell & Vermeulen have all made important contributions in the field of 'sustainable' design. Major players such as Foster, Rogers and Kohn Pedersen Fox (KPF) are pursuing research into low-energy buildings (Foster's Swiss Re tower, Rogers's Lloyds' Registry of Shipping and KPF's Heron Tower project in London all reflect progressive thinking in terms of energy use), but British legislation in this area is permissive to a degree and North American dependence on mechanical servicing has become standard practice in the office sector.

Recent projects such as Caruso St John's New Art Gallery Walsall, Herzog & de Meuron's Tate Modern and Long & Kentish's National Maritime Museum Cornwall exhibit both a strong sense of 'materiality' (a fashionable quality) and a matter-of-factness that eschews strong form in favour of 'as found' minimalism. The 'new simplicity' characteristic of much recent Swiss architecture has certainly had a marked influence in Britain. The work of Herzog & de Meuron (before its Tate Modern coup), Gigon & Guyer, Morger & Degelo and, supremely, Peter Zumthor has inspired many younger British architects.[10] The architecture of those senior British figures John Pawson, David Chipperfield and Tony Fretton depends on an artist's feeling for the quality of materials and expertise with the management of light and space rather than any structural gymnastics or visual surprises, and their approach has influenced a number of younger practices. In contrast, the 'Blobmeisters' and other advocates of striking form create buildings that are effectively huge works of sculpture (and painting, given the taste for strong colour). It is anyone's guess how far this fashion will be reflected on the streets of Britain, although both Libeskind's 'Spiral' for the Victoria and Albert Museum, London, and Alsop's Fourth Grace will be unmissable landmarks. Herzog & de Meuron's Laban Centre in south-east London is one of the most notable European buildings of the early century, a sensuous supershed responding to (and yet transforming) its riverside setting and forming a creative 'village', complete with streets and squares, within its colourful container. The Laban confirmed the position of the Swiss practice among the international first division.

When James Stirling died in 1992, reducing the 'big three' in Britain to two, many asked: who are the stars of the future? Two aspirants have since achieved this status, Alsop and Hadid. There are other contenders. No architect in Britain today gets more publicity from the fashionable media than David Adjaye, whose sense of drama is almost baroque, whose use of materials is sensuous and yet

Caruso St John's New Art Gallery Walsall (2000), housing the Garman Ryan Collection, is typical of many regenerative projects funded by the National Lottery. Its matter-of-fact minimalism responds directly to its location in a former industrial area.

disciplined. Adjaye's first big building is eagerly awaited. Meanwhile, Foreign Office Architects, the partnership of Farshid Moussavi and Alejandro Zaera-Polo, has completed a very big (and very fine) building in the Japanese port of Yokohama, which few in Britain will see. Moussavi is by origin Iranian, Zaera-Polo Spanish, yet they came together in London. Britain is an entrepôt of architectural talent, serving the world, but architects are also faced with the challenge of addressing the needs of a small, crowded island that some of their predecessors managed to deface badly. The projects in this book suggest that architects in Britain relish this challenge. Back in the 1980s 'pluralism' was a much-discussed issue. Now it is a reality. British architecture is diverse, contentious and very much alive and kicking.

1 D. Sudjic, *Norman Foster, Richard Rogers, James Stirling, New Directions in British Architecture*, London 1986, p.191.

2 J. Summerson, introduction to T. Dannatt, *Modern Architecture in Britain*, London 1959, p. 28.

3 See M. Glendinning and S. Muthesius, *Tower Block*, London 1994.

4 Introduction to C. Amery and D. Cruickshank, *The Rape of Britain*, London 1975, p. 7.

5 C. Jencks, *The Language of Post Modern Architecture*, London 1977, p. 101.

6 Rowe and Koetter's "Collage City" was published in the *Architectural Review* in August 1975.

7 See A. Saint, "Commentary", in *Allies and Morrison*, Michigan Architecture Papers, 2, Ann Arbor 1996.

8 *Building Design*, 19 July 2002.

9 W. Alsop, "Years of neglect mean we have a country fit for nothing", *The Architects' Journal*, 9 January 2003, p. 20.

10 See *A Matter of Art: Contemporary Architecture in Switzerland*, Basel 2001, for an up-to-date survey of the Swiss scene.

BARNSLEY MASTERPLAN, BARNSLEY, SOUTH YORKSHIRE
ALSOP ARCHITECTS

FOURTH GRACE, PIERHEAD, LIVERPOOL
ALSOP ARCHITECTS

GATESHEAD MILLENNIUM BRIDGE, GATESHEAD, TYNE AND WEAR
WILKINSON EYRE ARCHITECTS

GLASGOW HARBOUR MASTERPLAN, GLASGOW
KOHN PEDERSON FOX

KENT MESSENGER MILLENNIUM BRIDGE, MAIDSTONE, KENT
STUDIO BEDNARSKI

MANCHESTER INTERNATIONAL CONVENTION CENTRE, MANCHESTER
STEPHENSON BELL/SHEPPARD ROBSON

NEW ISLINGTON, MANCHESTER
ALSOP ARCHITECTS

PENARTH HEADLAND LINK, GLAMORGAN
PATEL TAYLOR

PICCADILLY GARDENS, MANCHESTER
TADAO ANDO

SCOTTISH PARLIAMENT, EDINBURGH
EMBT/RMJM SCOTLAND

BARNSLEY MASTERPLAN
BARNSLEY, SOUTH YORKSHIRE

ALSOP ARCHITECTS, 2001–

Will Alsop's regenerative masterplan for the centre of Barnsley aims to transform a neglected industrial town into a densely populated and vibrant regional centre. The project addresses problems created by post-war planning, which generated an obtrusive ring-road and sterile areas of surface parking, and aims to put Barnsley on the tourist map.

Barnsley is an ancient borough and market town, but during the last two centuries its economy has been dominated by one industry: coal mining. The complete closure of the South Yorkshire coalfield during the 1980s hit the town hard. The establishment of Yorkshire Forward as a regional development agency produced the support that the local authority needed to develop a new vision for Barnsley in the twenty-first century. Alsop Architects was commissioned late in 2001 to develop a regeneration strategy for the town centre. Aspirations were high: the council leader told Will Alsop that the aim should be to make Barnsley a place that every foreign tourist would want to visit. (Not such a far-fetched idea: how many tourists went to the industrial city of Bilbao before the opening of the Guggenheim?)

Alsop's starting-point was to seek out the views of local people; a series of workshops brought together many groups in the community. Despite its problems, Barnsley inspires strong feelings of loyalty, and there were clear ideas of what sort of changes were needed. For Alsop, the town centre had great strengths in terms of its historic buildings and range of activities but was increasingly blurred at the edges, where it faded into a drab zone of ring roads and warehouse sheds. His response was to propose the designation of a central zone as clearly circumscribed as a walled town within which new development – residential, retail, offices, cultural and educational – would be concentrated. Alsop envisaged a new 'wall' of building around the circumference of the central area, with up to ten storeys of mixed-use space and 'gateways' marking points of arrival. New parkland around the perimeter will reconnect Barnsley to the surrounding countryside, with fingers of green extending to the very heart of the town. The historic market is to occupy a prime position in the recast centre.

The idea of Barnsley as an Italian hill town might seem outlandish, but it helped to spark off a wider debate about the town's future. Alsop's advocacy of the town as a place of immense interest and potential helped dispel scepticism. In summer 2002 Alsop's vision of the walled city was exhibited at the Venice Biennale. The masterplan was subsequently further developed to form the basis for planning policies affecting the town centre. What was ridiculed by some as a mere joke could begin a dramatic change of fortunes for the town.

The high-profile developer/architect competition for a major new building at Liverpool's Pierhead – a 'fourth grace' to stand alongside the Port of Liverpool, Cunard and Royal Liver buildings – produced a shortlist of four. In December 2002 Will Alsop's proposal was chosen over those by Edward Cullinan, Norman Foster and Richard Rogers. It was set to be refined and developed during the course of 2003, in consultation with the city community.

The project is unashamedly an attempt to put Liverpool, a city known for its wealth of Georgian and Victorian buildings, on the modern architectural map. Backed by the North West Development Agency, which could underwrite it financially, the Fourth Grace is rather more than an unrealistic aspiration. Alsop's mixed-use scheme would certainly give Liverpool an unmissable new landmark. As proposed in the competition entry, it contains 340 flats, a 107-bed hotel, about 8000 square metres (86,000 square feet) of offices and 5000 square metres (54,000 square feet) of shopping, plus a new museum space and conference/exhibition facilities. A "24 hour, 365 days a year experience" is promised. The architecture certainly expresses the essential dynamism of the city. This could be the British equivalent of the Yokohama ferry terminal, Japan.

The development consists of a number of distinct elements: the Hill is a large multi-purpose conference/exhibition space that also houses a permanent space for the National Museums and Galleries on Merseyside. "Hovering" above (Alsop's term), the Cloud contains the hotel, with bars, restaurants and viewing gallery on top. The apartments (the Living) are located in a striking eighteen-storey building, almost as tall as the Liver Building, to the rear of the site. The development extends out to the banks of the River Mersey, with the Edge forming a low-rise, transparent 'garden of light' and housing shops, cafés, studios and other facilities, plus a new terminal for the famous Mersey ferry. New public transport and pedestrian connections are envisaged, as well as a landscape project to embrace the adjacent docks and generate an integrated waterfront linked to the nearby Albert Dock, a tourist magnet that contains the Tate Liverpool.

Liverpool's post-1945 decline has left the city a poor relation of the regional capital, Manchester, where new architecture reflects a lively civic and business culture. The Fourth Grace could be the shot in the arm that Liverpool needs.

Opposite
Will Alsop's project for a 'fourth grace' on the famous pierhead at Liverpool was a key component of the city's winning bid to become European Capital of Culture 2008.

Right
The section through the scheme clearly shows the division into conference and exhibition spaces topped by a hotel and viewing gallery, with an eighteen-storey apartment building to the rear.

GATESHEAD MILLENNIUM BRIDGE
GATESHEAD, TYNE AND WEAR

WILKINSON EYRE ARCHITECTS, 1997–2001

"But is it really architecture?" some asked when Wilkinson Eyre picked up the Royal Institute of British Architects' 2002 Stirling Prize – for the second year running – with the Gateshead Millennium Bridge. The question was quite irrelevant, although the architects acknowledge the major contribution made to the project by structural engineer Gifford & Partners. The success of the bridge is symbolic, quite apart from its practical agenda of connecting the opposing banks of the River Tyne and allowing the regeneration process to spill over into long-neglected Gateshead. Like Antony Gormley's monumental sculpture

The Angel of the North, it has become a local icon, something truly extraordinary and transformational inserted into a familiar (and sadly jaded) local scene. Chris Wilkinson, Jim Eyre and colleagues have been adopted as honorary north-easterners.

The practice was commissioned after a competition in 1997, on the basis of its previous bridge designs. The bridge was a vital link to the two other regenerative projects being undertaken by Gateshead Council on the riverside – the BALTIC arts centre (see pp. 44–45) and the Foster-designed Sage music centre (see pp. 114–15).

The quays along the Tyne are no longer commercially significant, but vessels still pass along the river and the bridge had to provide a clear channel for them while being accessible and inviting to pedestrians. It was the idea of making the process of opening into a genuine spectacle, by day or night, that sets the project apart. The bridge itself consists of a pair of arches: one forms the deck, with separate routes for pedestrians and cyclists, while the other supports the deck on cables. The arches pivot to allow boats to pass, the whole bridge tilting in a motion that has been compared to the opening of a giant eye.

The idea of a bridge as a symbolic monument is hardly new – Tower Bridge in London is a classic example of engineering clothed in architecture – but here it was given a new boost by the work of the architect–engineer Santiago Calatrava, who was responsible for a striking 1990s bridge on the Salford riverside. The new Gateshead bridge might seem a mannered exercise compared to its local precursors, the High Level and Tyne bridges, but its delicacy not only reflects the minimalism possible with modern materials and technologies, but equally provides a piquant visual contrast to the solid strength of industrial Tyneside.

Left
One of a series of dramatic bridges connecting Newcastle and Gateshead, the Millennium Bridge uses modern design and construction technology to create a lightness of effect that contrasts with the monumentality of its historic predecessors.

Opposite
The bridge is designed for use by pedestrians and cyclists, and separate routes are provided for each. The pedestrian route is slightly elevated to give clear views along the river. A computerized lighting programme allows for an infinite range of dramatic effects by night, when the structure emerges as an ethereal but dramatic presence in the riverside scene.

GLASGOW HARBOUR MASTERPLAN, GLASGOW

KOHN PEDERSEN FOX, 1998–

The Clyde is a majestic river, comparable to the Danube as it flows through Budapest, yet Glasgow, even more than London, has for centuries turned its back on its river. The banks of the Clyde were, of course, dominated by the warehouses of the port and by heavy industry, notably shipbuilding, which survived the clearance campaigns of the post-war era but has now largely vanished, leaving large areas of redundant, blighted 'brownfield' land.

Norman Foster's convention centre was a marker for the regeneration of the riverside in the 1990s. The Glasgow

Harbour masterplan by Kohn Pedersen Fox continues the process of renewal westwards along the Clyde – a former industrial area tightly contained by massive railway embankments and by the more recent Clydeside Expressway. (The salubrious residential quarter of the West End, with the main campus of Glasgow University and the city's Museum and Art Gallery at Kelvingrove, is on the far side of this barrier.)

The aim of the masterplan is to integrate the riverside with the rest of the city, extending the grid of the West End towards

the Clyde by bridging over the motorway and removing redundant railway tracks. New transport connections include rail stations, pedestrian and cycle routes, and a projected tram link. The stress is on high density – that of the West End – with buildings on a scale appropriate to the riverside, and mixed use. Some 3000 residential units are planned, together with offices, shops, hotels and leisure facilities, interspersed with public squares and gardens – a total of around 326,000 square metres (3,500,000 square feet) of accommodation.

The various elements in the masterplan have been the subject of design competitions, and a number of practices have already been appointed. The first phase of development is scheduled for completion in 2004. In tandem with such projects as BDP's Glasgow Science Centre and David Chipperfield's BBC Scotland headquarters at Pacific Quay (see pp. 216–17), Port Glasgow reflects the city's rediscovery of the riverside. Within a decade, the banks of the Clyde could become a major centre of activity, a destination for Glaswegians and outside visitors alike.

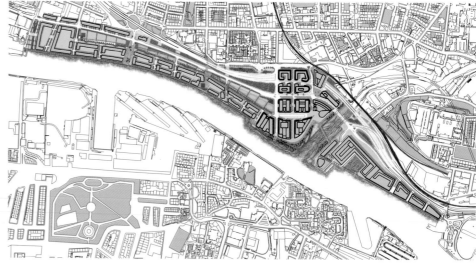

The model and site plan show clearly the development of the new urban quarter on former industrial land along the Clyde, to the west of Glasgow city centre. The masterplan aims to extend the city's West End, with its established residential and cultural character, down to the river.

Architecture or engineering? With the increasing involvement of such architects as Norman Foster, Wilkinson Eyre and Lifschutz Davidson in the design of bridges, the question is frequently asked. The role of the architect is, however, clear: that of defining form and then working with the engineer to achieve that form in an efficient and practical way. Both must be in balance; when form is at odds with function, the results can be bizarre. (Or sublime: think of Tower Bridge, a far from 'functional' solution to the brief, but in consequence a symbol of London rather than just a means of crossing the Thames.) It is the elegance

and economy of Cezary Bednarski's Maidstone bridge that sets it far apart from a purely functional approach to spanning the River Medway.

The context is a new landscaped park developed along the banks of the Medway, close to the centre of Maidstone (the county town of Kent). Bednarski was responsible for both bridges that provide connections across the river. The 101.5-metre (333-foot) Kent Messenger Millennium Bridge, designed in collaboration with engineers Stráský, Husty & Partners, is claimed as the world's first cranked stress-ribbon bridge, constructed on a dogleg alignment in

response to the physical context of the steep river banks, with their groups of mature trees. Sufficient height was required to allow for the passage of pleasure craft.

Stress-ribbon bridges consist of concrete planks resting on steel cables, a straightforward and economical idea – the suspended walkway is the structure – but one dependent on precise structural formulae. The appeal of this construction method is that there is no need for the masts, cables, props and dampers necessary when other structural strategies are used. The walkway is therefore clear of obstructions except for perimeter railings.

Bednarski admits that the design of the bridge "was driven as much by the single-minded desire to push the limits as it was by landscape qualities of the site". Cranking the span creates particularly demanding structural problems, but also a dynamism and bravura that a straightforward span would lack. Lighting is accommodated within the deck, lending the bridge a glowing presence at night. The staircase from the river bank, giving access where the deck changes direction, provides intermediate structural support but is a delightful feature in itself. In this bridge, at least, architecture and engineering are in harmony.

A prop provides the only intermediate structural support for this highly innovative pedestrian bridge: a minimal solution that avoids the cables and masts of many recent small-scale bridges.

MANCHESTER INTERNATIONAL CONVENTION CENTRE, MANCHESTER

STEPHENSON BELL/SHEPPARD ROBSON, 1994–2001

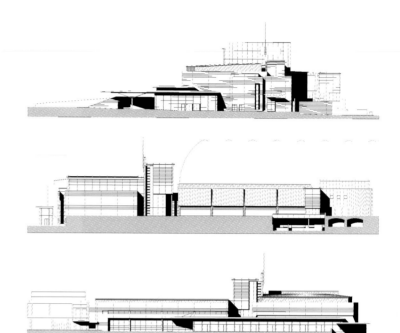

The process of urban renaissance needs landmark structures, such as the Gateshead Millennium Bridge, The Lowry in Salford, or the Imperial War Museum North in Manchester, but there is an even more pressing need for projects that are about repair and reinstatement. Stephenson Bell is a practice with a notable track record in this field; indeed, Roger Stephenson pioneered the new bar and loft culture of Manchester, and the city's Smithfield Buildings, converted for Urban Splash, remains a classic case of recycling.

The Manchester International Convention Centre, Stephenson Bell's most important new-build scheme to date, was designed in collaboration with Sheppard Robson. If it fails to excite, blame it on the *genius loci*. A previous generation of Manchester architects participated eagerly in the sack of the Victorian city at a period when issues of conservation and context were low priorities. The convention centre is an unashamedly contextual, though contemporary, building that successfully fills a yawning gap in the fabric of the city centre.

The site was railway territory from the 1880s to the 1960s. Manchester Central was the last of the big passenger termini to invade the city. It was surrounded by a large goods yard, of which the 1890s Great Northern warehouse was the centrepiece. After the site was abandoned, the buildings stood derelict. The great arched shed of the station was transformed in the 1980s into G-MEX, a huge exhibition centre. The warehouse has since been converted for retail use. The success of G-MEX generated the convention centre, which occupies the gap between the two buildings.

Extensive use of red sandstone cladding connects the centre to its context. Its form is strong, but not strident. The brief was for an 800-seat auditorium, with the usual ancillary facilties, plus a large multi-purpose hall. Compositionally, the two spaces are connected by a linking tower containing plant, lifts, staircases and WCs. The new public spaces around the building are well handled, and a backwater has been incorporated into the city centre. It is unfortunate, however, that the interiors contain a certain amount of embarrassingly crass detail, which reflects the dependence of the project on a design-and-build contract.

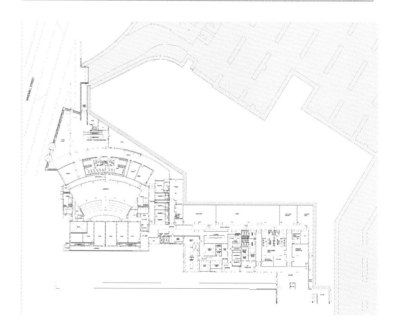

Above
The building occupies a narrow slot between the former Central Station, now G-MEX, and the monumental Great Northern warehouse, and contains an auditorium and multi-purpose hall.

Right
Red sandstone cladding responds to the historic context of central Manchester, and particularly to the brick-and-terracotta bulk of the Midland Hotel.

NEW ISLINGTON, MANCHESTER

ALSOP ARCHITECTS, 2002–12

The Ancoats and Miles Platting districts of Manchester, east of the rejuvenated city centre, were creations of the Industrial Revolution. Around the Rochdale and Ashton canals mills, workshops and dense formations of housing for those working in them formed a new townscape that impressed (and appalled) such foreign visitors as Karl Friedrich Schinkel and Friedrich Engels. After the Second World War, most of the housing in this area was progressively demolished, as the population of 100,000 was reduced by more than 90%. Surviving industrial buildings are, ironically, now regarded as of international significance and are being recycled as part of the Ancoats Urban Village project.

East Manchester is now the principal focus for Manchester's continuing regeneration campaign. The development of SportCity around the 2002 Commonwealth Games site has been a significant impetus for the renewal process. The New Islington project, a partnership between Manchester City Council, English Partnerships and developer Urban Splash, aims to develop a new, sustainable urban community on the site of the existing Cardroom estate, a 1970s development consisting of low-rise houses around *culs-de-sac*, which is now a crime-ridden 'sink estate' lacking shops and other amenities and any source of employment. New Islington will contain housing for the existing population plus newcomers – 1400 homes in all, with a mix of tenures – together with workshops and offices, shops, pubs, school, nursery, health centre, community hall and 93,000 square metres (1,000,000 square feet) of parks and gardens. Improved transport links, including a Metrolink stop, will end the isolation of the area from the rest of the city.

Fundamental to the project is the development of the canal system, including the reopened Rochdale canal, to create a city on water with a strong identity. As masterplanner, Alsop Architects has infused New Islington with a memorable vision of urban living and engaged the local community, which is desperate for change, in its realization. Some of the buildings are being designed by Alsop, others are being commissioned from a variety of practices in line with the masterplan. Development takes the form of medium-rise blocks along fingers of canal opening off a new canal basin; this connects the two existing canals and is the focus for the new community facilities, including a school, health centre and rowing club. Some existing buildings, including parts of Ancoats hospital, are retained and refurbished or converted to new use.

The 'sustainable' agenda at New Islington is more than window-dressing. Boreholes will provide a locally sourced water supply. Houses and apartments are heavily insulated and serviced by a combined heat and power plant, partly fuelled by gas produced from recycled sewage.

If all goes to plan, New Islington will be a model of an environment-friendly, socially integrated, mixed-use urban quarter developed to a density in line with Urban Task Force prescriptions. Alsop has, however, given it a dimension that extends beyond the realm of urban regeneration and social renewal. If the architecture lives up to the images generated when the project was launched, this will be a showplace of new design to match anything in Europe.

The New Islington masterplan creates an urban quarter of water and green space as part of a strategy to regenerate an area where post-war housing has proved a failure physically and socially. The development, involving private and public investment, is intended to be mixed in terms of both use and composition.

PENARTH HEADLAND LINK, GLAMORGAN

PATEL TAYLOR, 2002–05

The Cardiff Bay barrage is a considerable engineering achievement, though its long-term effects on the ecology of the bay remain to be seen. Regrettably, however, Will Alsop's vision of the barrage as a fusion of engineering, architecture and landscape remained unrealized and the completed structure is functional but lacking in visual delight.

Just west of Cardiff, the Edwardian pier at Penarth manages to succeed where the late twentieth century failed. Recently restored, the pier stands at one end of Patel Taylor's new promenade, which extends around the rocky headland to a new harbour forming the westward termination of the barrage. The Headland Link will allow pedestrians to walk from Cardiff's Pierhead (site of the forthcoming Wales Millennium Centre and Welsh Assembly building) to the attractive seafront in Penarth.

Working with engineer Techniker, Patel Taylor devised a structural formula for the connection that is both functionally efficient and extremely elegant, with an emphasis on economy of means in the best tradition of seaside architecture. At the west end, a new timber-decked esplanade replaces an ugly 1960s car park. The remainder of the link consists of precast concrete paving slabs on a draped steel framework, the whole 700-metre (2,300-foot) length supported on just eight concrete columns, textured and coloured as a response to the setting of sombre sandstone cliffs. The undulating form of the link has a relaxed flow, in tune with the natural context and reflecting the way in which architecture and engineering can work together to achieve a highly expressive effect.

Wrapping round Penarth headland, the new, gently undulating walkway connects the Victorian resort of Penarth with the Cardiff Bay barrage and the rejuvenated pierhead area of Cardiff. Supported on piers sunk into the shoreline, the Headland Link offers a contemporary take on the nineteenth-century pier.

PICCADILLY GARDENS, MANCHESTER

TADAO ANDO, 1999–2002

Piccadilly Gardens is more clearly identifiable as the 'heart' of Manchester than is Albert Square. However, while the latter is dominated by Alfred Waterhouse's magnificent town hall, Piccadilly Gardens is surrounded by a very mixed bag of buildings, with the huge 1960s Piccadilly Plaza development a dominant (and rather brutish) presence. The square was created when the old infirmary was demolished in 1909, but in recent years it has degenerated into a rather squalid place, with rundown gardens, in which some fine public statuary was randomly disposed, adjoining a bus station. The advent of trams in the 1990s only added to the confusion.

This confusion has now been banished – or at least rationalized – as part of a radical make-over of the square in which the Japanese master Tadao Ando collaborated with EDAW and Arup Associates. A substantial new mixed-use development now occupies the eastern edge of the space, giving a clearer sense of enclosure. The new layout of the square, however, is strikingly open, in contrast to the sunken, heavily planted gardens of the past, which were hard to police. The square is now on a level with surrounding streets; its landscape has been kept simple: grass, stone paving, trees, oak benches and restored statuary. The character of the space is defined by the contrast of straight and curving geometries. An oval fountain, in which water jets spurt straight from the pavement, and the pavilion adjoining the revamped tram station, provide the principal interventions. This is a very fine piece of concrete construction, meticulously detailed and crying out for some public use, rather than the retail units it contains.

Above
Formerly the site of the city's infirmary, Manchester's Piccadilly Gardens has become the focus of the modern city centre and is a major transport interchange.

Opposite
The first building in Britain designed by Tadao Ando (*bottom right*) displays his trademark use of concrete, employed in a spirit quite different from that of the 1960s Piccadilly Plazza scheme (*top right*) in the background.

SCOTTISH PARLIAMENT, EDINBURGH
EMBT/RMJM SCOTLAND, 1998–2003

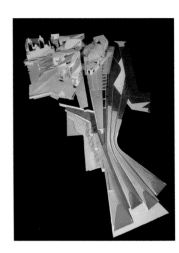

The referendum on devolution, which was held in 1997, led to the establishment of the Scottish Parliament. The selection, the following year, of the Barcelona partnership of Enric Miralles and Benedetta Tagliabue (EMBT), working in collaboration with Edinburgh-based RMJM, to design the parliament's new building close to Holyrood Palace seemed to augur well, suggesting that Scotland was looking beyond its own boundaries for a symbol of self-government. The project has since been marked by continuing controversy, however, focusing on the rising cost of the building – even by late 2002 some commentators were putting the final price at about £400,000,000. The tragic death of Enric Miralles cast a further cloud over the saga.

The competition-winning scheme was based on a belief that the parliamentary building should not be a conventional monument – Edinburgh has more than its share of these – but a structure 'sitting in the land' and reflecting the character of the entire nation. Native Scottish materials, including granite, slate and oak, featured prominently in the designs. Given the complexity of the scheme, initial estimates of its cost were certainly optimistic. The project has been realized using construction management, with a consequent element of redesign in an attempt to rein in costs.

The low-rise form of the building is equally in tune with an agenda of openness and accessibility: traditional hierarchies and institutional forms are eschewed in favour of an explicitly informal diagram. The debating chamber, the heart of the complex, is elevated above the landscape, which is allowed to invade the site. Other functions are grouped in a series of towers around the eastern edge of the site, close to the historic Queensberry House garden. The members' offices are placed along the western perimeter, forming a continuation of the historic grid pattern of streets and buildings off the High Street. Despite the modifications to Miralles's original concept, the interiors look set to be genuinely memorable and an expression of a radical vision of government. The building is claimed as a model of sustainability, with natural ventilation, solar panels for power and the use of 'grey' water for WCs and irrigation of the surrounding landscape, itself designed to encourage biodiversity.

The controversy over the parliamentary building ranks with that over London's Millennium Dome for intensity and sheer bitterness. Many Scottish architects feel that the project has cast a blight on their profession. This is certain to be an interesting and provocative building, despite the difficulties that have beset the project. But whether it will provide twenty-first-century Scotland with a clear and generally comprehensible symbol of nationhood remains to be seen.

Above
The extraordinary, organic form of the building responds to its context, on the edge of the Old Town, close to Holyrood Palace.

Opposite
The interiors, flowing, light-filled and finely crafted, offer a new image for democracy but have been achieved at a controversially high price.

ARTIST'S HOUSE, ROCHE COURT
NR SALISBURY, WILTSHIRE
MUNKENBECK & MARSHALL

BALTIC, GATESHEAD, TYNE AND WEAR
ELLIS WILLIAMS ARCHITECTS

BATH SPA, BATH, SOMERSET
NICHOLAS GRIMSHAW & PARTNERS

BLACKWELL, WINDERMERE, CUMBRIA
ALLIES & MORRISON

BOATHOUSE 6, PORTSMOUTH, HAMPSHIRE
MacCORMAC JAMIESON PRICHARD

DARWIN CENTRE, THE NATIONAL HISTORY MUSEUM
SOUTH KENSINGTON, LONDON SW7
HOK INTERNATIONAL

THE DEEP, KINGSTON UPON HULL, HUMBERSIDE
TERRY FARRELL & PARTNERS

DOWNLAND GRIDSHELL, WEALD AND DOWNLAND
OPEN AIR MUSEUM, SINGLETON, WEST SUSSEX
EDWARD CULLINAN ARCHITECTS

EDEN PROJECT, NR ST AUSTELL, CORNWALL
NICHOLAS GRIMSHAW & PARTNERS

GLASGOW SCIENCE CENTRE, GLASGOW
BUILDING DESIGN PARTNERSHIP

HORNIMAN MUSEUM EXTENSION, FOREST HILL
LONDON SE23
ALLIES & MORRISON

IMPERIAL WAR MUSEUM NORTH, STRETFORD
MANCHESTER
DANIEL LIBESKIND

LANDFORM, SCOTTISH NATIONAL GALLERY
OF MODERN ART, EDINBURGH
CHARLES JENCKS/TERRY FARRELL & PARTNERS

LONGSIDE GALLERY SCULPTURE BARNS
WAKEFIELD, WEST YORKSHIRE
BAUMAN LYONS ARCHITECTS/TONY FRETTON ARCHITECTS

MANCHESTER CITY ART GALLERY EXTENSION
MANCHESTER
HOPKINS ARCHITECTS

MILLENNIUM GALLERIES AND WINTER GARDEN
SHEFFIELD, SOUTH YORKSHIRE
PRINGLE RICHARDS SHARRATT

MOUNT STUART VISITOR CENTRE, ISLE OF BUTE
MUNKENBECK & MARSHALL

NATIONAL MARITIME MUSEUM CORNWALL
FALMOUTH, CORNWALL
LONG & KENTISH

THE QUEEN'S GALLERY, BUCKINGHAM PALACE
LONDON SW1
JOHN SIMPSON & PARTNERS

RSA PLAYFAIR PROJECT
NATIONAL GALLERY OF SCOTLAND
AND ROYAL SCOTTISH ACADEMY, EDINBURGH
JOHN MILLER & PARTNERS

SUTTON HOO VISITOR CENTRE
WOODBRIDGE, SUFFOLK
VAN HEYNINGEN & HAWARD

THE TURNER CENTRE, MARGATE, KENT
SNØHETTA & SPENCE

VISITOR FACILITIES, PAINSHILL PARK
NR COBHAM, SURREY
FIELDEN CLEGG BRADLEY

WHITBY ABBEY VISITOR CENTRE AND MUSEUM
WHITBY, NORTH YORKSHIRE
STANTON WILLIAMS

THE WOMEN'S LIBRARY, WHITECHAPEL, LONDON E1
WRIGHT & WRIGHT ARCHITECTS

WYCOLLER VISITOR CENTRE, NR COLNE, LANCASHIRE
HAKES ASSOCIATES

YORKSHIRE SCULPTURE PARK VISITOR CENTRE
WAKEFIELD, WEST YORKSHIRE
FEILDEN CLEGG BRADLEY

ARTIST'S HOUSE, ROCHE COURT
NR SALISBURY, WILTSHIRE

MUNKENBECK & MARSHALL, 2000–01

Munkenbeck & Marshall's first building at Roche Court, a Regency house, was completed in 1999: an exquisitely detailed and structurally ingenious gallery space slotted into a gap between the house and a nineteenth-century conservatory. Roche Court is the home of the New Art Centre (NAC), with its constantly changing outdoor display of twentieth-century and contemporary sculpture; the gallery houses smaller and more fragile works. The Artist's House was commissioned by the NAC's director, Madeleine Bessborough, in 2000.

The idea of the Artist's House is, to some degree, a conceit. In theory, it is a house, with kitchen and bathroom, in which an artist could live for a time; in practice it forms a domestic setting for the display of art – "a beautiful house full of beautiful things" – inspired in part by Kettle's Yard in Cambridge.

The site was a gap, occupied by a derelict shed, in the former stable yard behind the house; the brief included extending one of the staff residences in the converted buildings around the yard.

Intrinsic to the project was the creation of a new visitor route around the site, to which the public has always been admitted, free of charge, on a very informal basis. The context demanded a solid aesthetic rather than the slender minimalism of the gallery. The house is faced in render, with a pitched roof clad in recycled slate. Its proportions are essentially Classical, with a *piano nobile* level containing the principal spaces, and the bedroom and bathroom below. The top-lit living-room, with its coved ceiling and full-height frameless glazing, is the heart of the house. The furnishings were designed by the architects and, together with the timber floors, give warmth and texture to the interiors.

Conceit it may be, but the Artist's House, open to all, provides a model for middle-class housing in the countryside far removed from the typical developer's neo-Georgian or neo-Tudor box. It equally reflects a vision of the country house as a cultural generator that is all too rare in the 'heritage culture' of Britain.

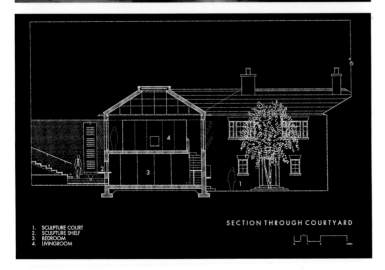

1. SCULPTURE COURT
2. SCULPTURE SHELF
3. BEDROOM
4. LIVINGROOM

SECTION THROUGH COURTYARD

Left
The Artist's House (not intended for regular occupation but rather a gallery space) fills a gap in the stable court of a Regency country house.

Opposite
The render walls and slate roof defer to the context, but the interiors are uncompromisingly modern and filled with natural light, an inspirational setting for the changing display of works of art. Many of the furnishings were specially designed by the architects.

With 3000 square metres (9840 square feet) of gallery space, BALTIC is seen as an 'art factory' rather than a museum in the conventional sense. The monumental concrete structure, which formerly housed grain silos, had to be gutted, and now houses a continually changing display of works. The all-glazed eastern elevation offers superb views of the Gateshead Millennium Bridge from its top-floor viewing box.

Like Wilkinson Eyre's Stirling Prize-winning Millennium Bridge (see pp. 28–29) and Foster and Partners' forthcoming Sage music centre (see pp. 114–15), the BALTIC centre for contemporary art is a key component in the regeneration of Gateshead's quayside. (The process is, of course, a spin-off from the successful renaissance of Newcastle's waterfront – the Millennium Bridge provides the connection – and its impact on Gateshead as a whole remains to be seen.) Dominic Williams of Ellis Williams Architects, a sizeable but little-known practice from the North West, won the competition for the conversion of the former Baltic flour mill in 1994, although the project took a painful eight years to come to fruition thanks to delays with Heritage Lottery funding.

The brief was to provide a series of spaces for the changing display of contemporary art (the BALTIC has no permanent collection but hosts temporary exhibitions), plus the usual visitor facilities. Like London's Tate Modern, however, the BALTIC is also visited by those attracted more by the place and its sociable ethos, and the views out, than by the contents. Director Sune Nordgren describes it as an "art factory" where artists can interact with the building.

The raw material offered no internal space to compare with Tate Modern's huge turbine hall. It was filled with 148 concrete grain silos and had to be gutted as a first step towards reuse, with only the external skin retained, which was no mean task for structural engineer Atelier One. The distinctive corner towers were utilized for plant, staircases and service lifts. Three glass lifts provide the principal means of access to visitors – there are no escalators – and serve five levels of gallery space plus the rooftop restaurant, a prefabricated capsule craned into position. The display spaces are sensibly diverse in character and far more attractive than those in Tate Modern. From a number of points in the building, including a top-floor viewing box, there are fine views across the river and surrounding conurbation. A low new-build extension to the west houses a bar, brasserie, shop and reception area.

If the quality of the detailing is surprisingly variable and sometimes inconsistent, the idea of a factory for art has been effectively realized. In a region where many lives have been blighted by the rapid rundown of such traditional industries as mining and shipbuilding, the BALTIC suggests that the legacy of industry can be put to positive use.

BATH SPA, BATH, SOMERSET

NICHOLAS GRIMSHAW & PARTNERS, 1997–2003

In contrast to so many of the Heritage Lottery-funded projects of the 1990s, the Bath Spa project aimed to capitalize on the existing (albeit neglected) resources of a place rather than create new 'attractions' of limited value and dubious long-term viability. Bath has been a spa city for at least 2000 years. The Romans developed it as a centre for self-indulgence and relaxation, as well as therapy, a tradition revived in the eighteenth century when Bath became a focus for fashionable society, the warm springs providing water both for drinking and for bathing.

The twentieth century saw the steady decline of the spa, and many of the facilities were closed on health grounds. Bathing stopped in 1978. At the same time, Bath prospered as one of Britain's prime tourist destinations and a jewel of 'the heritage'; public revulsion at the demolition of hundreds of Georgian buildings during the 1960s led to blanket protection for the entire historic core. Not surprisingly, Bath was not a place to go in search of good modern buildings: (generally weak) pastiche was the rule for new development.

Nicholas Grimshaw's £21,000,000 project has finally restored Bath's status as a spa, following the failure of a number of commercially funded proposals during the 1980s and 1990s. Its blend of restoration and innovative new design is a shot in the arm for a city in danger of being stifled by its own past while losing sight of the asset that brought it into being.

The raw material for the project was a group of six buildings at the heart of the city. The striking new spa building, which replaces the 1920s municipal swimming pool on Beau Street, takes the form of a free-standing cube, clad in Bath stone, set within a glazed enclosure. The new open-air pool is located at roof level, with fine views for bathers over the city. The adjacent Georgian hot bath has been refurbished as a special treatment and therapy centre. The Grade I-listed Cross Bath (on the site of an ancient cistern) has been renovated, with sensitive new interventions, as a place for bathing open to all; to qualify for Lottery support the project had to guarantee access to local people. The town house at 7/7A Bath Street, also Grade I, has been converted into a ticket office, restaurant and visitor centre, and the former Hetling pump room into an interpretive and educational facility and offices for the spa.

In many European countries, spas are popular resorts for the sick and the healthy, a tradition that has largely evaporated in Britain. Perhaps Bath will lead the way towards its revival.

BLACKWELL, WINDERMERE, CUMBRIA

ALLIES & MORRISON, 1996–2001

A major work by the great Arts and Crafts architect M.H. Baillie Scott, Blackwell is a classic 'artistic house' by a master whose work was known and imitated throughout Europe (Hermann Muthesius, author of *Das Englische Haus*, particularly admired the house). Blackwell was completed in 1900 as a holiday retreat for a Manchester brewing magnate; during the Second World War it became a boarding school, and it was later insensitively converted into offices. Although under-maintained, the Grade I-listed house fortunately did not suffer irrevocable alterations during this period of decline. In 1996 the first moves were made to acquire and restore Blackwell as a showpiece in its own right and as a gallery for exhibitions on arts and crafts themes.

Following the acquisition of Blackwell by an independent trust in 1999, Allies & Morrison's task (under associate Diane Haigh, an authority on Baillie Scott's work) was to repair the fabric, strip off later accretions, restore lost decorative details and finishes, and make the building work as a modern museum. A shop, café, education spaces and offices all had to be accommodated, together with modern services, and a visitor route created through the house. Inevitably, there was a tension between the demands of conservation and those of reuse; disabled access, for example, was a high priority. A number of functions were incorporated within the former service wing, which stands at a right angle to the main body of the house.

Blackwell is now entered in the angle between the two wings. This is not an entirely satisfactory arrangement, as Baillie Scott's interiors form a progression from the original entrance porch, but it is one that allows for wheelchair access (with a new lift to the first floor) and the creation of a generous new ticketing and retail area. The principal ground-floor rooms – the drawing-room, hall and dining-room – have been carefully restored to their original state; missing details were replicated. The main bedrooms, above, serve as galleries for temporary exhibitions. In some places the new environmental and security services inevitably intrude, but they had to be admitted if the building was to fulfil its new function. For some critics, the magic of Blackwell has been diminished, yet the project has given the house an assured future. It involved some hard decisions, but on occasions these have to be made.

Top
Opening Blackwell to the public meant identifying a suitable point of access in the angle between the main part of the house and the service wing.

Opposite and above
New interventions are kept minimal and sympathetic to the spirit of the original building.

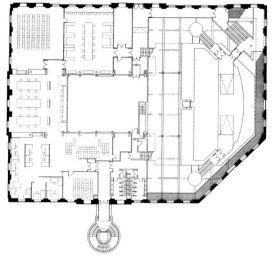

BOATHOUSE 6, PORTSMOUTH, HAMPSHIRE

MacCORMAC JAMIESON PRICHARD, 1997–2001

The extraordinary versatility of MacCormac Jamieson Prichard (MJP) – ranging from university buildings, a huge reconstruction of Broadcasting House and an extension to the Science Museum, to one of the best of the Jubilee line extension stations, at Southwark (all three in London) – continues to impress. The practice is admirable both on the macro and the micro scale, and working with history is one of its strengths.

Any British practice engaged in historic buildings work has to establish a dialogue with English Heritage, which can be either constructive or deeply frustrating. With a few caveats, however, English Heritage was supportive of MJP's radical proposals for Boathouse 6, which is not only a listed building, but also a scheduled ancient monument.

The building's status reflects the importance of Portsmouth dockyard in British history. In recent years, the 'historic' dockyard – the Royal Navy's 'working' dockyard is a secure area – has become a major tourist attraction run by an independent trust. The brief for Boathouse 6 involved provision of an interactive visitor facility, cinema, café and shop, plus accommodation for the maritime studies department of Portsmouth University. The building, dating from 1843 and used for storing and repairing small boats, had been damaged by wartime bombing and rather crudely repaired.

The destruction of part of the monumental iron frame of the building provided a slot for the new 275-seat auditorium, which sits in the space like the hull of a warship, structurally independent of the historic fabric. The new use necessitated the introduction of stairs, lifts and services; raised floors were inserted, served by frankly expressed perimeter ducts. A fully glazed lift and stair tower provides access to the university accommodation on the second floor. Permanent interventions are of a solid metallic character, in tune with the original. Transient elements, such as the café, are treated as 'furniture' and executed in timber. It is the clear philosophical basis of this scheme that sets it apart: its rationale is in tune with the work of the Victorian engineers.

Accessibility and the provision of modern services were the key issues in the adaptation of the historic Boathouse 6 at Portsmouth dockyard as a visitor facility and a university department of maritime studies. The partial destruction of the building's iron frame in the Second World War allowed the auditorium to be inserted (*opposite, top right*).

DARWIN CENTRE, THE NATURAL HISTORY MUSEUM
SOUTH KENSINGTON, LONDON SW7

HOK INTERNATIONAL, 1992–2002

HOK's Darwin Centre, which opened in autumn 2002, is the latest addition to the densely developed museum and education quarter of South Kensington, London. The building stands west of Alfred Waterhouse's Grade I-listed Natural History Museum, the Science Museum's recent Wellcome Wing (by MacCormac Jamieson Prichard) is a close neighbour, and Imperial College's packed campus lies just to the north. The HOK building is, in fact, the first phase of the Darwin Centre. Phase Two, won in competition by Danish practice C.F. Møller Architects, is scheduled for completion by 2007, replacing a very utilitarian inter-war laboratory block.

The Darwin Centre project reflects The Natural History Museum's role as a place of research – it employs 350 scientists – as well as an educational and visitor facility. Its Spirit Collection contains up to 22,000,000 zoological specimens preserved in alcohol and gathered over the last 200 years; some were brought from Australia by Captain Cook in 1768. The collection was previously housed in extremely inadequate premises, which were inaccessible to the public.

The 12,000-square-metre (130,000-square-foot), £21,000,000 centre reflects the museum's aim to open up the collections more widely to the public and to foster interest in its research work. It combines three functions: a store for the specimens, laboratories for researchers and controlled access for visitors (up to fourteen guided tours are run daily). The building is divided into three zones reflecting its mixture of roles. To the north is an eight-storey climate-controlled store. The south side of the centre contains laboratories and offices; visitors can see scientists at work from the connecting walkways along the side of the central atrium, which forms the heart of the building.

HOK's architecture is well judged in its relationship to Waterhouse's masterpiece. The centre is clearly subsidiary to the main museum building, and has a tough, almost industrial quality: internal finishes are far from extravagant. A visual connection to Waterhouse, however, is provided by the use of terracotta panels to frame the fully glazed southern façade. Supported on specially cast brackets (deliberately zoomorphic in appearance), the outer façade is a *tour de force* in itself. Behind it, the inner skin of the building is screened by sun-tracking louvres that close down when the sun strikes directly on the south front. The roof is formed partly of ETFE (ethyltetrafluoroethylene) panels, which provide effective insulation while allowing daylight to penetrate the atrium.

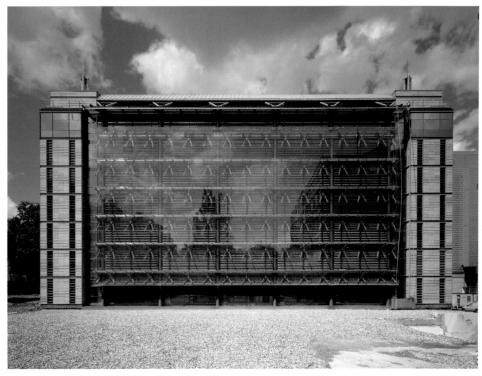

THE DEEP, KINGSTON UPON HULL, HUMBERSIDE

TERRY FARRELL & PARTNERS, 1998–2002

Opposite and below, left
The building is conceived as an extrusion of the seabed, its prow jutting into the Humber estuary near the mouth of the River Hull.

Below, right
Inside, visitors follow a ramped route, formed between enormous tanks in which sea life can be glimpsed at close quarters.

Terry Farrell is an enigmatic figure, on one level a phenomenal success (knighted and with many built projects, in Britain and abroad, to his name), yet arguably underrated and widely misunderstood. The rejection of The Deep in Kingston upon Hull for a Royal Institute of British Architects award in 2002 was symptomatic: locally popular, the project has proved a major tourist draw. Farrell sees the building as a restatement of the radical ideas that drove his work during his fifeen-year partnership with Nicholas Grimshaw (1965–80). Too often Farrell is typecast as a Post-modernist on the basis of a few built projects of the 1980s – all on prominent London sites – although Post-modern styling was a reflection of a wider disenchantment with the Modern Movement.

The Deep is certainly striking, both in form and location. The site, at the confluence of the rivers Hull and Humber, was formerly a shipyard, and the decline of Hull's maritime industries has driven the regeneration programme of which The Deep is a symbol. Farrell was commissioned for the project in 1998. The idea was to create not an aquarium (a collection of fish tanks) but a 'submarium' relating "the story of the oceans from the past to the present and into the future". The building and its contents had to be a dramatic voyage of discovery.

Comparisons with Frank Gehry's Guggenheim Bilbao are rather absurd. There was none of the extravagant budget of the latter: Farrell's building cost a mere £20,000,000; cladding is in marine-grade aluminium rather than titanium; and, despite Heritage Lottery funding, an enabling development of business units on part of the site was necessary to balance the books. Nor does The Deep have the ethereal lightness of Gehry's masterpiece – deliberately so. The building was planned as an extrusion of the seabed, with the geological strata expressed as jagged layers in the structure. The tanks it contains hold 13,000 litres (2850 gallons) of water, so that a heavyweight structural frame was needed.

The visitor route, from the top downwards, is a dramatic ramp through the interstices between the tanks. Only in the restaurant and viewing area, which occupy the 'beak' of the building overlooking the Humber, does the route break out into daylight. Farrell was obviously aware that an eye-catching landmark was wanted, but he managed to retain something of the tough industrial quality of the site. The Deep is no more arbitrary in form than Shankland & Cox's nearby tidal barrier (1980), a structure with which it successfully competes for attention.

DOWNLAND GRIDSHELL
WEALD AND DOWNLAND OPEN AIR MUSEUM
SINGLETON, WEST SUSSEX

EDWARD CULLINAN ARCHITECTS, 1995–2002

Below, left and middle
The Gridshell sits happily in its rural Downland setting. The cladding has been produced from local woodlands.

Below, right, and opposite
The structure is made of green oak thinnings, a natural and renewable resource used in a highly innovative way that would have been inconceivable without computer design techniques.

Edward Cullinan Architects, the practice that Ted Cullinan (born 1931 and formerly an associate of Denys Lasdun) founded four decades ago, is a perennially youthful and optimistic outfit, and this building shows the practice on top form. A concern for context and history, a passionate interest in materials and a sincere commitment to environmental issues have characterized Cullinan's work over the years. The so-called Downland Gridshell at the excellent Weald and Downland Open Air Museum (which rescues and re-erects endangered timber-framed buildings from the south-east of England in a striking parkland setting)

reflects all these concerns, fusing them with an entirely contemporary approach to the creation of expressive form.

The brief was to create a sturdy, daylit space for the conservation and repair of historic building components that could also be open to the public, plus a store for the museum's extensive archive of artefacts, tools and furniture, and a small display area. The solution could have been a repro-barn, practical and inoffensive. The client's wish to demonstrate the vitality and relevance of the vernacular tradition in the twenty-first century produced instead the commission to Cullinan, who worked with engineer Buro

Happold and expert specialist contractors. Heritage Lottery funding made it possible to start construction in 2000.

The Downland Gridshell is part of a continuum with the collection of historic buildings at Singleton (the oldest dates from the fourteenth century), yet its intricate form could not have been designed without present-day computer technology. The stress is on sustainability. The slender, curved laths that form the structure are made of green oak thinnings from French plantations. The green cedar cladding comes from local woodlands. Virtually nothing was wasted. Two layers of aluminium foil

enclosing 25 millimetres (1 inch) of foam provide effective insulation. Glazing is low-cost polycarbonate. The archive store and display area are contained within a concrete box, set into the sloping site. Heating in winter is supplied by a domestic boiler.

The Downland Gridshell is a joyful structure, ingenious in engineering terms and a work of handmade craftsmanship in a great tradition. But it is equally an inventive piece of architecture that, as Cullinan insists, "takes us back to our roots" and makes the case for a new way of building forged from natural materials without mass-production processes.

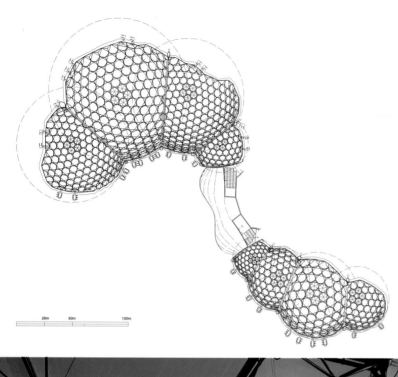

EDEN PROJECT, NR ST AUSTELL, CORNWALL

NICHOLAS GRIMSHAW & PARTNERS, 1995–2001

Grimshaw's Eden Project has transformed an eyesore – an abandoned china clay quarry – into one of the biggest visitor attractions in the South West. The linked biospheres are covered in ETFE, a material far lighter, more flexible and cheaper than glass. The concept is a series of intersecting spheres, expressed as domes at surface level.

Cornwall has the image of a romantic place apart, as the land of *Frenchman's Creek* and summer holidays. But there is another Cornwall, which the Eden Project addresses: a place of industry. Around St Austell the landscape is littered with spoil tips created by the china clay industry. The site for Eden was a huge worked-out clay quarry, 500 metres (1640 feet) across.

Nicholas Grimshaw & Partners (NGP) was approached in 1995 by the project's founder, Tim Smit, who was impressed by Grimshaw's new Waterloo International terminal in London. Eden opened in 2001, the budget having risen to £86,000,000. It has been an enormous popular success, attracting hordes of visitors to an area that was previously off the tourist track.

The brief was to create "the largest plant enclosure in the world", with plants from all over the globe growing in specially tempered conditions. The initial proposal was to build an enormous glasshouse, a vast modern version of the nineteenth-century palm house at Kew. However, the problematic nature of the site – uneven and potentially unstable – brought about a dramatic change of direction, and instead panels of ETFE (ethyltetrafluoroethylene) foil were substituted for glass as the cladding for the twin 'biomes', the larger of which

has a maximum internal height of 55 metres (180 feet). ETFE is light (1% of the weight of glass), transparent and durable, and was therefore ideal for the task in hand.

The basic idea of the project, which involved a typically close collaboration between Grimshaw and engineers Anthony Hunt & Partners, is that of a series of intersecting domes. Apart from the biospheres, NGP was responsible for an earth-roofed link building and for the visitor centre, which forms the point of entry to the site. The latter uses low-energy natural materials, including rammed earth, gabions (metal cages of rocks reclaimed from the site) and timber cladding, which would once have seemed incongruous in a Grimshaw building. But Eden has moved the High-tech agenda forward by revisiting the visions of Buckminster Fuller, the progenitor of High-tech, who once proposed covering all of Manhattan with a biosphere.

If the sheer popularity of the project, and the layer of tourist tat it has spawned, detract somewhat from the quality of the place, Eden has to be recognized for the extraordinary, indeed startling, achievement that it is. Whether it proves to be an eccentric experiment or the model for a new approach to environmental management remains to be seen.

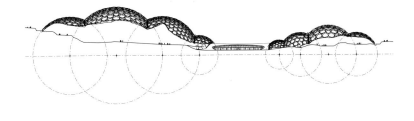

GLASGOW SCIENCE CENTRE, GLASGOW
BUILDING DESIGN PARTNERSHIP, 1995–2001

Building Design Partnership (BDP) is the sleeping giant of British architecture. Although the largest of all British practices, with 800 staff and offices in London, in major provincial cities and around Europe, its character is oddly elusive. Is BDP just another commercial practice, or does it aspire to something more? In the 1980s the firm drifted into Post-modernism with the rest, while Norman Foster stuck to his guns, and it has managed to combine commercial muscle with critical acclaim.

The Glasgow Science Centre is one of a number of recent BDP projects that suggest that the practice has set its sights firmly on design excellence. BDP won the competition for the development in 1995. The site is a focus of regeneration in the post-industrial wastelands along the River Clyde; Foster's 'armadillo' exhibition and conference centre is just across the river and David Chipperfield's BBC Scotland headquarters (see pp. 216–17) is set to rise near by.

Included in the £75,000,000 scheme is the tower originally designed by Richard Horden for a city centre site and relocated here with minimal adustments to the Horden designs. It is a pure folly, rotating with the wind and providing twenty-five visitors at a time with views over the city. The science centre itself is a classic Lottery project, stuffed with interactive gadgetry in

5000 square metres (54,000 square feet) of gallery space over five floors, plus lecture theatres, a planetarium, a teaching laboratory and workshops that provide educational back-up for the gadgets. A separate building houses Scotland's first IMAX cinema, together with restaurant and function facilities.

The use of titanium as a cladding material invites comparisons with Frank Gehry's Guggenheim Bilbao, and the science centre is indeed a more modest expression of the ongoing preoccupation with memorable architectural form. Surrounded by water – actually a moat against vandals – the main block is often compared to an upturned ship, perhaps a conscious reference to a lost local industry. At Bilbao, the internal spaces arguably do not quite live up to the promise of the stunning exterior shell. The science centre, in contrast, is internally luminous; unlike the usual 'black box', it has a fully glazed north wall looking out to the city centre. The basic qualities of the scheme have survived unfortunate budget cuts (reflected in some below-par finishes in places) so that there is none of the disjunction between container and fit-out common in projects of this kind. A low-energy servicing strategy completes the winning formula for one of the best of the science-based Lottery schemes.

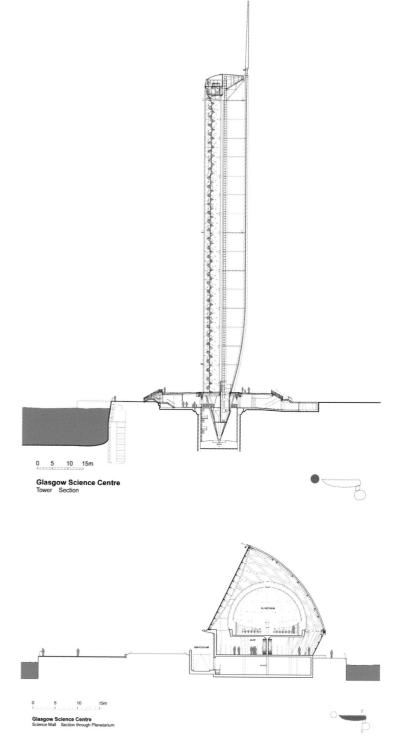

Glasgow Science Centre
Tower   Section

0   5   10   15m

Glasgow Science Centre
Science Mall   Section through Planetarium

0   5   10   15m

Above
Section of the viewing tower and science centre.

Opposite
Its form resembling an upturned ship, reflecting the local shipbuilding tradition, the science centre is clad in titanium with a fully glazed northern elevation looking out on to the city centre.

HORNIMAN MUSEUM EXTENSION
FOREST HILL, LONDON SE23

ALLIES & MORRISON, 1995–2002

The Horniman, tucked away in the south London suburb of Forest Hill, is one of the most idiosyncratic of the capital's smaller museums in terms of both its architecture and its contents (a mix of ethnography, stuffed animals and musical instruments). It is a well-loved local institution, established for "the recreation, instruction and enjoyment" of south Londoners, but it is not on the tourist trail. Its original building, however, opened in 1901, is a remarkable and – for Britain – unusual example of the Art Nouveau style, designed by Charles Harrison Townsend for philanthropist founder Frederick Horniman.

The museum stands next to a public park, also created by Horniman, but until the completion of the Allies & Morrison scheme it turned its back to the park, with an entrance only from the busy London Road. Allies & Morrison was commissioned to develop expansion plans in 1995. The brief was to provide a new gallery for temporary exhibitions, an education centre, café and shop. Issues of accessibility had to be addressed as part of a major development programme that also saw the repair and refurbishment of the original building. The decision was taken to reorientate the museum so that the main entrance is now from the park.

Allies & Morrison's extension, stone-fronted and with a metal-clad curved roof, takes its form and scale from Townsend's original: to the gardens, for example, it is faced in red brick. Inside, a daylit, double-height space provides access to all parts of the building. The café, shop and education rooms are at ground level, with the new galleries, including a space specially designed for displaying musical instruments, below (actually at street level, since the slope on the site is quite dramatic). To the north, the building opens up to a paved court, where a restored Victorian conservatory provides a venue for social events, and to the park beyond.

This is a finely crafted, highly sensitive scheme that integrates old and new painlessly and brings light and air to the mysterious world of the Horniman. Not that the character of the original has been diluted: it is still possible to use Townsend's entrance, up steps from the street. The amenities of the museum, which is a real community asset, have been vastly improved and a Victorian institution given a new lease of life.

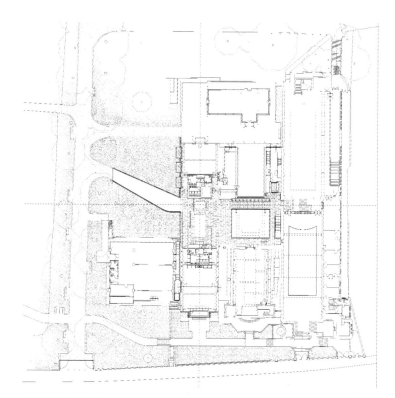

Above
Allies & Morrison's carefully considered extension takes its cue in terms of scale and materials from Townsend's original building of 1901.

Opposite
The extension is arranged around a double-height space from which café, shop, education spaces and new galleries can be accessed.

WORLD

CONFLICT

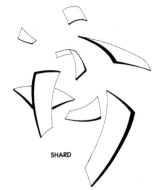

SHARD

MUSEUM

IMPERIAL WAR MUSEUM NORTH
STRETFORD, MANCHESTER

DANIEL LIBESKIND, 1997–2002

The first built work by Daniel Libeskind in Britain, the Imperial War Museum North is, in fact, only the third completed building anywhere by the architect (although the Spiral project at the Victoria and Albert Museum, London, looks increasingly likely to be realized). Libeskind won the competition for the new museum in 1997, when his now-famous Jewish Museum in Berlin was finally under construction after years of delay. Sited in Stretford, close to the Manchester United football ground but outside the city of Manchester, the museum opened in summer 2002.

Libeskind, who was born in Poland into an Orthodox Jewish background, is a controversial architect whose deeply felt work sets out to touch the emotions and even to shock. The location for the new museum, a branch of the parent institution

in London, is in the extensive (and now redundant) dockland area created by the opening of the Manchester Ship Canal in the late nineteenth century. Michael Wilford's Lowry arts centre, which draws on the 'deconstructivist' aesthetic of Libeskind, Zaha Hadid and others, is just across the water in Salford. Other new development in the area is, regrettably, ordinary or even banal in quality – a sadly lost opportunity. The budget for the new museum (around £28,000,000, with the building itself costing about £15,000,000) was modest in comparison with that of the Jewish Museum (let alone the superstar regenerative museum, Frank Gehry's Guggenheim Bilbao). This is reflected in a simple steel and concrete structure, far from glamorous aluminium cladding and generally robust detailing.

The client's brief was for a building illustrating the theme of conflict in the twentieth century and beyond, but, with the idea of urban regeneration equally to the fore, a landmark was required. Libeskind has certainly created an eye-catcher. The building is conceived as three interlocking 'shards' representing earth, air and water – the theatres in which modern wars are conducted and three of the four elements. (The fourth, fire, is omnipresent in a museum of war.) The shards can be seen as parts of a shattered globe. The earth shard, with its gently curved floor, contains the museum space proper, with its displays illustrating the way in which wars affected the lives of ordinary people in the north of England. The dramatic air shard forms the point of entry to the building, with its projected images, suspended planes and missiles,

and education spaces. The water shard curves down towards the water of the canal and houses a restaurant, café and performance space.

Libeskind is an architect who sets his architecture in a strongly philosophical and polemical context, and many critics have responded to it in equally philosophical vein. Yet this building exemplifies the straightforward architectonic power of the work, transforming ordinary materials and an uneventful site into a place of memorable quality. Libeskind feels that the lesson of recent history is that the world is threatened by order and disorder alike: "By navigating the course between rigid formalities on one hand, and the chaos of events on the other, this building reflects an evolving identity open to profound public participation, access and education."

Robustly detailed and economically constructed, the museum forms a striking if disturbing presence on the dockside opposite Michael Wilford's Lowry arts centre in Salford. The thinking behind the designs draws on ideas of destruction and dissolution resulting from war.

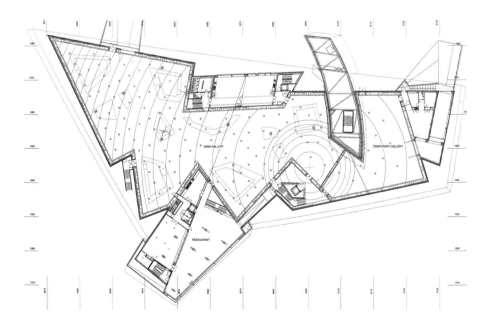

LANDFORM
SCOTTISH NATIONAL GALLERY OF MODERN ART
EDINBURGH

CHARLES JENCKS/TERRY FARRELL & PARTNERS, 1995–2002

Informed by Charles Jencks's concern to merge scientifc theory with landscape design, the Landform has transformed the space in front of the Scottish National Gallery of Modern Art, formerly one of Edinburgh's 'pauper palaces'. On a small scale, it continues a great British tradition of creating landscapes with sculpted earth and water.

Terry Farrell's conversion of the former Dean Orphanage in Edinburgh (a Category A-listed building by Thomas Hamilton, completed in 1833) to house modern works, including important bequests of Surrealist art, from the collections of the National Galleries of Scotland was completed in 1999. The Dean is one of Farrell's most compelling projects, transformational and yet highly sensitive to its historic setting and capitalizing, through the almost theatrical use of light and colour, on the natural drama of Hamilton's interior spaces.

Across the road is another of Edinburgh's 'pauper palaces', the former John Watson's Institution, a noble Neo-classical structure now housing the Scottish National Gallery of Modern Art (NGMA). The Dean project generated a masterplan for the surrounding area, including the Dean cemetery and the banks of the Water of Leith. Architect, critic and patron Charles Jencks was invited to design a Landform for the hitherto featureless grounds of the NGMA, drawing on themes already seen in the landscape of the garden in Dumfriesshire that he designed with his late wife, Maggie Keswick.

Completed in summer 2002, the Landform consists of a sinuous turfed mound enclosing three small lakes and offering a site for the display of large sculptures. It reflects both the essential character of Edinburgh, a city where an unforgettable natural setting of sea and mountains frames one of the world's finest urban ensembles, and Jencks's interest in chaos theory and fractal geometry as sources of new architectural form, its romantic informality contrasting with the sombre Classicism of the architectural setting.

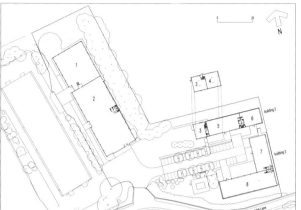

1 Sculpture Gallery
2 Sculpture Gallery
3 Café
4 Studio/Workshop
5 Studio/Workshop
6 Studio/Workshop
7 Sculpture Restoration
8 Studio/Workshop

LONGSIDE GALLERY SCULPTURE BARNS
WAKEFIELD, WEST YORKSHIRE

BAUMAN LYONS ARCHITECTS/
TONY FRETTON ARCHITECTS, 2000–03

The Yorkshire Sculpture Park was established in 1977 at Bretton, near Wakefield. Feilden Clegg Bradley's visitor centre (see pp. 88–89) is the central element in the development of the core landscape-park site close to Bretton Hall. The acquisition of 96 hectares (237 acres) of land at Longside, on the edge of the park, however, has greatly increased the scale of the operation and provided scope for future growth.

The conversion project for a group of three former barns at Longside was completed in 2001 by Leeds-based Bauman Lyons Architects. The utilitarian modern farm structures were converted into a 615-square-metre (6600-square-foot) sculpture gallery (the first show was of the work of Sir Anthony Caro), studios, workshops and cafés. Only the portal frames of the existing buildings were retained; they were simply reclad using fair-faced concrete blocks, externally rendered, and provided with extensive glazing to capitalize on fine views. The result is a very satisfying and practical environment for the display of art works and products of the 'creative industries'.

Tony Fretton was commissioned to fit out space in one of the barns to house the Arts Council's entire sculpture collection and associated works on paper, which has long been in store in a number of locations. From Bretton, works are loaned to museums and galleries in Britain and abroad; in addition a small and changing selection is put on display there. A conservation workshop is also provided. Security and the creation of an appropriate environment for conserving art works were key elements in the brief: climate-controlled spaces had to be created, using the thermal mass of structure rather than artificial cooling. The low-cost project displays Fretton's customary attention to detail and instinctive feeling for the nature of materials.

A group of modern farm buildings, approximately 1.5 kilometres (1 mile) from the sculpture park visitor centre (see pp. 88–89), was converted to gallery and workshop space in 2001 as part of an economical project by Bauman Lyons. More recently, one of the barns has been adapted by Tony Fretton to house the Arts Council's sculpture collection.

MANCHESTER CITY ART GALLERY EXTENSION
MANCHESTER

HOPKINS ARCHITECTS, 1995–2002

Opposite
The new atrium, with staircase and lifts, forms
part of an extension linking the former Manchester
Institution building with the Athenaeum, and
occupying a former car-park site.

Above
The staircase is an elegant exercise in the carefully
detailed High-tech manner with which Hopkins
was formerly associated.

The advent of the National Lottery has
produced a wave of entirely new museums
and galleries around Britain, such as
Tate Modern in London, the BALTIC at
Gateshead (see pp. 44–45), the Millennium
Galleries in Sheffield (see pp. 70–71), the
Imperial War Museum North in Manchester
(see pp. 64–65) and The Lowry in Salford.
In most cases these Lottery-funded projects
have been linked to an agenda of economic
regeneration and are located in areas hit
by the decline of traditional industries.
Investing in Britain's long-established
regional museums is a less fashionable
cause, yet many, dependent on local
authorities for funding, are in desperate
straits. The major expansion of Manchester
City Art Gallery (which did secure Lottery
support) is a pointer to what can be
achieved with these venerable institutions.

Hopkins Architects won the competition
for an extension to the gallery in 1995.
The City Art Gallery is housed in Charles
Barry's Grade I-listed, Neo-classical
Manchester Institution on Mosley Street,
completed in 1823. The Athenaeum (also
by Barry), around the corner in Princess
Street, is a former gentlemen's club, which
was acquired by the gallery some years
ago. The site for the new building is a
former car park to the rear of these two
buildings, bounded by Nicholas Street
and George Street. The project included
a comprehensive restoration of the historic
buildings, undertaken by Peter Inskip and

Peter Jenkins Architects, which addressed
issues of disabled access, substantially
upgraded visitor facilities and reinstated
historic colour schemes.

The diagram of the scheme is pleasingly
rational, with a new atrium, containing lifts
and stairs, as the hub of the linked complex
of buildings. There are new subsidiary
entrances from Princess Street and Nicholas
Street, although the main entrance remains,
quite properly, on Mosley Street. The
Athenaeum, which was ill-connected to the
old gallery, is now entered from the atrium
space. The new building contains galleries
at first- and second-floor level, with
education spaces, a lecture room, loading
bay and store on the ground and basement
levels. Externally, the extension defers to
its imposing neighbours; in any case it
addresses distinctly secondary streets. The
façades are formed of limestone panels set
in a concrete frame, and circular staircases,
clad in glass brick, punctuate the masses
on George Street. The galleries' coffered
ceilings are in precast concrete, executed
with Michael Hopkins's usual attention to
detail and incorporating natural and artificial
lighting. Hopkins is sometimes criticized for
an alleged preoccupation with context and
history that obscures the essential
modernity of his architecture. The rigour
of this project, which recalls the exquisite
David Mellor building (1990) at Butler's
Wharf in south-east London, suggests that
this critique is something of a generalization.

MILLENNIUM GALLERIES AND WINTER GARDEN
SHEFFIELD, SOUTH YORKSHIRE
PRINGLE RICHARDS SHARRATT, 1996–2002

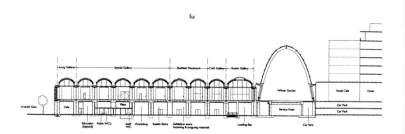

Sheffield is one of a number of major British cities where the scale and form of post-1945 reconstruction has proved problematic and a perceived disincentive to new investment. The praise that such critics as Nikolaus Pevsner and Ian Nairn heaped on the post-war centre (the consequence of wartime bombing) now seems ill judged. In reality, faceless new buildings and intrusive highways created a hostile environment, and businesses opted for Nottingham, Leeds and Manchester rather than Sheffield.

Pringle Richards Sharratt was appointed to design the Millennium Galleries and Winter Garden in 1996, in the context of a masterplan (subsequently modified by Koetter Kim) by Terry Farrell for what has become known as the Heart of the City project, with an emphasis as much on public space as new architecture. The galleries were constructed in 1999–2001; the Winter Garden was completed in 2002. The two buildings form part of a new pedestrian route between the railway and bus stations and the civic quarter around the impressive late Victorian town hall. The site for the Winter Garden includes part of that of the failed 1970s town hall extension, now demolished.

The Millennium Galleries occupy a sharply sloping site parallel to Surrey Street and close to Sheffield's central library, Graves Art Gallery and two theatres.

This generates a two-level section: the restaurant, stores, services and other ancillary spaces are at undercroft level, while the galleries, housing a mix of permanent and temporary displays, are above. The galleries are accessed from a broad, daylit public 'avenue', which is open well into the evening. Top-lit, with exposed precast-concrete vaults on a strict grid, the gallery spaces reflect the influence of Louis Kahn. Engineers Buro Happold married form with function in terms of the low-energy servicing strategy, which utilizes the stack effect and the thermal mass of the concrete structure.

The galleries and avenue, cool and neutral in effect, form the preface to the striking Winter Garden, where the spectacular timber, steel and glass roof has affinities with the covered court in Michael Hopkins's Portcullis House, Westminster, London (for which John Pringle was partner-in-charge). The two linked buildings are credible components in the recast city centre: connectors more than isolated monuments. They look set to succeed where Branson Coates's Sheffield Pop Music Centre, an ill-advised attempt to do a Guggenheim Bilbao on the cheap, failed. Can the rest of the Heart of the City project maintain the high aspirations that they embody? If so, Sheffield really could be on the road to regeneration.

The Millennium Galleries and Winter Garden form a new covered route between the bus and railway stations and the civic quarter around the Town Hall. A public arcade leads to the spectacular steel, timber and glass Winter Garden, a benign covered space at the heart of a city disfigured by much post-war planning and development.

MOUNT STUART VISITOR CENTRE
ISLE OF BUTE
MUNKENBECK & MARSHALL, 1999–2001

Mount Stuart, the Victorian Gothic seat of the Marquesses of Bute on the Isle of Bute, could be called the San Simeon of Scotland – although in terms of architectural quality, if not hedonistic glamour, it beats Randolph Hearst's Californian pile hands down. The house and grounds first opened to the public in 1995 and now attract more than 30,000 visitors annually. The new visitor building was commissioned by Johnny Bute, the 7th Marquess, to replace more *ad hoc* facilities. Constructed in nine months, the building opened in June 2001 and incorporates ticket office, shop, WCs, audio-visual area and restaurant.

The site for the centre and adjoining car park is removed from the house and is seen as a public gateway to the estate – visitors walk from this point or use a courtesy bus service – which marks the transition from wild island landscape to cultivated aristocratic domain. Having bought a ticket, the visitor can walk straight through the building into the gardens, or linger to sample its attractions. The ground floor, sunk into the slope of the land, is a solid concrete structure clad with timber slats. The first-floor restaurant, seating 100, is a lightweight, fully glazed pavilion sitting on a 10-centimetre (4-inch) concrete slab.

The oversailing roof, which is built in timber and clad in aluminium, shelters an external terrace for summer meals.

This is a straightforward, far from extravagant structure (the total cost was £870,000) that manages to be sophisticated without being precious. The client set out to build "something special, and not compromise". With its elegance of form matched by immaculate detail, the building fulfils this ambition and shows Munkenbeck & Marshall at its best. One longs to see the practice take on a large new building.

The visitor centre sits at the entrance to the parkland around the Victorian mansion of Mount Stuart, almost one kilometre (half a mile) away. It contains the usual mix of shop, ticketing and restaurant area, and WCs. Above, the restaurant forms a glazed pavilion under a lightweight oversailing roof with striking views and shelter from the weather.

NATIONAL MARITIME MUSEUM CORNWALL
FALMOUTH, CORNWALL

LONG & KENTISH, 1996–2003

The new National Maritime Museum Cornwall strongly evokes the maritime vernacular of boatsheds, warehouses and lighthouses, and occupies a commanding position in the harbour. The interior of the building, skilfully daylit, accommodates a main gallery, 12 metres (40 feet) tall, a secondary gallery and subsidiary visitor and office spaces. The tower offers views across a harbour where shipbuilding and boat repairing remain important industries.

Formally opened early in 2003, the National Maritime Museum Cornwall is the latest of a series of out-stations of national museums sited in the regions: Evans & Shalev's Tate St Ives was an earlier example. The core collection of the new museum is an assembly of 140 historic small boats owned by the National Maritime Museum, London, but stored for many years in a south London warehouse and inaccessible to the public. The collections of the local maritime museum in Falmouth have also been subsumed by the new institution, which was largely funded by the Heritage Lottery Fund.

Falmouth remains a working port, with shipbuilding and repair an important local industry, so the waterfront museum has clear relevance to the local community as well as appeal to the visitors that the town seeks to attract. Long & Kentish's unfussy and pleasingly understated building is in tune with its unpicturesque setting; the commercial development of cinema, shops and housing that forms the remainder of an ambitious regeneration package will, it is hoped, possess similar qualities.

In essence, the building is a big shed, largely timber clad (with local oak) and slate roofed (albeit using a mono-pitch). Its straightforwardness recalls Caruso St John's New Art Gallery Walsall but in this instance it is a matter of common sense rather than artful referentiality. The lighthouse-like tower is the only concession to self-advertisement; some locals suggest that it should be brightly painted like a real lighthouse.

The heart of the building is the full-height (12-metre/40-foot), naturally lit gallery that houses most of the boats. A smaller, 'dark' gallery, set behind a hull-like wall, mixes real artefacts with projected film and video clips to illustrate the way in which the boats were used. The exhibition design, by Land Design Studio, seems well integrated with the architecture. Subsidiary galleries and ancillary spaces, including a shop and café, are stacked around the perimeter, like offices around a factory floor.

Designed by a practice formed out of the experience of Colin St John Wilson's British Library project in London, the National Maritime Museum Cornwall could hardly be more different from that county's other major Lottery venture, Nicholas Grimshaw's Eden Project (see pp. 58–59). One transports the visitor into an exotic world, far from the china clay pits in which it is sited; the other explores and reflects on living traditions that are echoed in its context. As Ian Nairn would have said: you pays your money and you takes your choice.

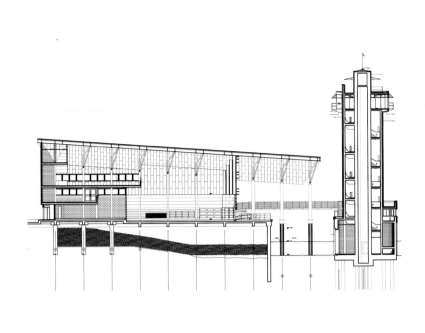

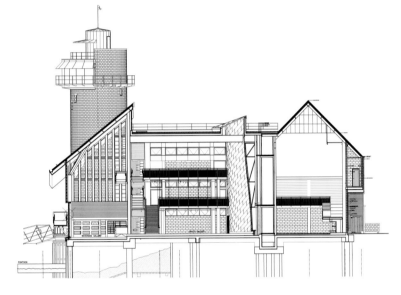

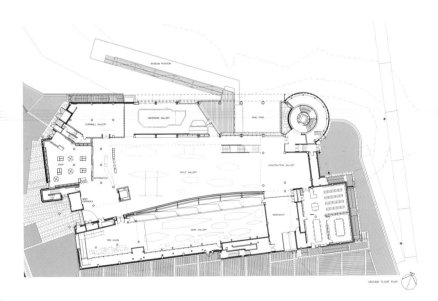

GROUND FLOOR PLAN

THE QUEEN'S GALLERY
BUCKINGHAM PALACE, LONDON SW1

JOHN SIMPSON & PARTNERS, 1997–2002

John Simpson's record as a committed supporter of the Prince of Wales's architectural campaigns might seem an obvious recommendation for this prestigious royal commission. The invitation list for the limited Queen's Gallery competition held in 1997 included, however, both Dixon.Jones and Hopkins Architects, practices whose take on history, although deeply felt, is far from literal. Hopkins had already designed the lightweight pavilion that caters for thousands of summertime visitors to Buckingham Palace.

The choice of Simpson was widely seen as a reflection of the conservative tastes of the royal family, yet the outcome is a building that declines to be merely deferential and in its flamboyance (and touch of excess) looks back to the heady days of the Prince Regent.

The original Queen's Gallery opened in a former stable block in 1962, but it was always an unworthy setting for the fabulous treasures in The Royal Collection. The implication was that the public could not be admitted to any part of the palace but must be kept in a separate corral, entered via an inconspicuous hole in the boundary wall. By the late 1990s, attitudes had changed so markedly that the new gallery was seen as a significant addition to the palace itself, with an imposing and inviting public entrance from the street and a connection to the Queen's apartments. Issues of security, conservation and accessibility were all addressed by the project.

In comparison with other great palaces Buckingham Palace is a lacklustre affair, yet the drab image imposed by Aston Webb's 1913 façade to The Mall conceals some handsome interiors, including state rooms by John Nash. The largest of the three new gallery spaces (which in fact sit on top of the palace kitchens, which were refurbished as part of the project) is an act of homage to Nash. Elsewhere, other heroes of the Classical tradition – Sir William Chambers, Sir James Pennethorne and Sir John Soane (the last a perennial source of ideas for Simpson) – provide inspiration. The pronounced entasis of the portico on Buckingham Gate draws on the model of the ancient Greek temples at Paestum, Italy.

Inside, the entrance hall features sculpture by the Scottish artist Alexander Stoddart. The staircase hall is a *tour de force*, with elaborate decoration in a Regency/Schinkelesque mode. Simpson is no more a purist than he is a minimalist. Decorative schemes throughout are richly colourful, an appropriate backcloth to some grandiose works of art. The overall effect is compelling. If there is a hint of vulgarity, it is perhaps deliberate: Simpson no more pursues 'good taste' than did Nash and the Prince Regent. This highly individual work of architecture is a significant product of the Royal Jubilee of 2002, although what it says about the monarchy and its cultural role today is hard to discern.

The portico on Buckingham Gate, inspired by the temples of Paestum, provides a dignified public entrance to the gallery. Inside, the gallery spaces draw on the example of Nash, Soane and other great Classicists, while the staircase hall perhaps evokes the excesses of the Regency.

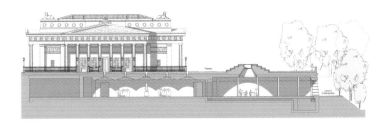

RSA PLAYFAIR PROJECT
NATIONAL GALLERY OF SCOTLAND
AND ROYAL SCOTTISH ACADEMY, EDINBURGH

JOHN MILLER & PARTNERS, 1999–2005

It is, in part at least, thanks to the architect William Henry Playfair (1789–1857) that Edinburgh acquired the title of 'the Athens of the North'. His monumental National Gallery and Royal Scottish Academy on the Mound, constructed over a thirty-year period, were key elements in the city's Neo-classical reconstruction. Although the National Gallery has undergone a major facelift since the 1980s under the directorship of Sir Timothy Clifford, it lacks space for temporary exhibitions and is short of the facilities – shops, restaurants and education spaces – now mandatory in large international museums. The adjacent Royal Scottish Academy was long used for temporary shows, but in recent years its "seriously dilapidated" condition has led to its effective closure.

The £29,000,000 Playfair Project, which John Miller won in 1999 over competitors including Terry Farrell and Dutch practice Mecanoo, finally gives the National Gallery the space and facilities it has long needed. The first phase, completed in summer 2003, consisted of the renovation of the academy building (now owned by the National Galleries of Scotland), when modern air conditioning, lighting and security equipment were installed and the historic fabric carefully repaired. In the second phase, due for completion in 2005, a more radical transformation will be achieved, with a new underground link beneath the two buildings containing a 200-seat lecture theatre, education rooms, restaurant, café, shop and cloakrooms. The fall of the site will give the National Gallery a new frontage to Prince's Street Gardens, which will become a major entry point. The link building will be faced in stone to match the Playfair buildings, to which it will be connected by staircases and lifts; a new entrance point for the works of art themselves will feature a door 7 metres (23 feet) high, faced in stone.

John Miller & Partners has a notable record in the refurbishment and extension of art galleries – its major extension to Tate Britain in London opened in 2001 – and there can be little doubt that this will be its most important project to date.

John Miller's Playfair Project finally integrates Edinburgh's National Gallery with the Royal Scottish Academy building, which the National Gallery now owns. A new subterranean connection contains lecture theatre, restaurant, education spaces and other facilities, and a new point of entry from Prince's Street Gardens.

In August 1939 a team of archaeologists made one of the most spectacular discoveries in the history of British archaeology on a site at Sutton Hoo, close to the River Deben, near Woodbridge in Suffolk. They unearthed the remains of a ship in which a king (or at least a great leader) had been buried, along with his treasure, in the seventh century. The treasure was subsequently taken to the British Museum; the site, containing a number of Saxon burial mounds, eventually came to the National Trust.

Visitor centres, like the historic sites they serve, come in all shapes and sizes. Van Heyningen & Haward's Sutton Hoo project was comparatively modest in cost and has an appropriate modesty of manner, reflecting these architects' genuine feel for the East Anglian vernacular. The site, set well away from the grave field itself, already contained an Edwardian house (converted into a study centre and flats) and stable block, with which the two new buildings by van Heyningen & Haward form a group. The larger of the pair is essentially an exhibition space, filled with rather distracting audio-visuals and graphics; the other houses the usual National Trust shop and café. The materials are simple: mostly timber, with some steel structural reinforcement and zinc-clad roofs. The quality of the buildings derives from careful detailing and sure proportions. Deeply overhanging eaves reinforce the impression that these are farm sheds; they mask the activities within from the surrounding fields, while allowing clear views out. The café has an external terrace with views over the river.

Van Heyningen & Haward is an experienced performer in historic contexts. This is one of the practice's best projects, characterized by an assured calmness and lack of special effects.

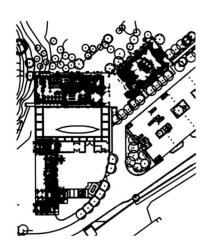

The visitor centre at Sutton Hoo, built of simple materials in a modern version of the rural vernacular, forms part of a group of estate buildings well away from the historic burial site. Overhanging eaves provide shade from the sun and allow the use of extensive glazing to capitalize on the wide views over the river and the surrounding countryside.

THE TURNER CENTRE
MARGATE, KENT

SNØHETTA & SPENCE, 2001–05

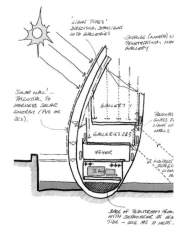

The concrete-framed Turner Centre, conceived as a giant pebble, sits in the water in the historic harbour of Margate. The top-lit interior contains gallery spaces connected by a ramp. The ticket office and other ancillary facilities are located on the harbour pier with a bridge into the galleries.

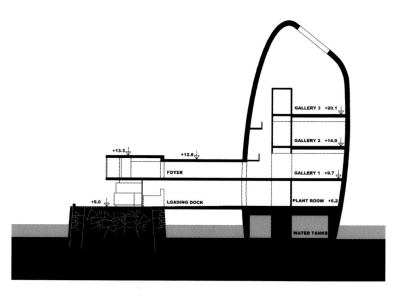

J.M.W. Turner, arguably Britain's greatest painter, frequently stayed in Margate, but there is nothing in the small Thames estuary resort to commemorate the fact. When the Turner Centre opens in 2005, Margate will be forcefully reminded of its illustrious visitor. The agenda behind the project is, however, about regeneration as much as commemoration. Margate is a far from wealthy town, and it needs to boost its image to attract more visitors and investment.

A high-profile competition was held in 2001 and won by the Norwegian Snøhetta practice working with Stephen Spence (formerly of Richard Rogers Partnership). The brief was for a landmark building that would also provide high-quality gallery space to contain a selection of Turner's work (Tate Britain, London, is to provide temporary loans) and a gallery for contemporary art (BritArt star Tracey Emin, for example, is a native of Margate).

The site is striking: the building is to be attached to the harbour pier, next to the old Custom House, with its foundations in the water. The structure must be stout enough to withstand exceptional storms. The concrete-framed building is clad in oak. Its top-lit interior is accessed by means of a ramp; the lofty top-floor gallery will be a particularly striking space. The ticket office, café and other ancillary facilities are located in a separate block on the pier, with a bridge link to the galleries.

VISITOR FACILITIES
PAINSHILL PARK, NR COBHAM, SURREY

FEILDEN CLEGG BRADLEY, 1997–2001

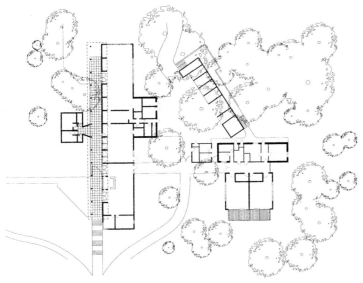

Visitor centres constitute a building type that, if not exclusive to Britain, reflects the British preoccupation with landscape, history and 'heritage'. Over the last thirty years the National Trust has developed a number of facilities of this kind, including, in most cases, a restaurant, shopping outlets, WCs and an exhibition area close to car parking. English Heritage's development adjacent to Whitby Abbey, North Yorkshire (see pp. 82–83), illustrates the increasing sophistication of visitor buildings on historic sites.

Painshill Park, near Cobham, Surrey, was laid out between 1738 and 1773 by Charles Hamilton, a pioneering Romantic who constructed a Gothic temple, hermitage, grotto, 'ruined abbey' and other evocative follies, virtually bankrupting himself in the process. The visitor centre at Painshill Park was commissioned by a small independent charity, the Painshill Park Trust. This was established in the 1980s to maintain and restore the landscape park, which had been rescued from dereliction by the efforts of the local authority.

Bath-based Feilden Clegg Bradley was commissioned to design the new centre in 1997; it was constructed in 2000–01. The site lies close to the walled kitchen gardens that served Hamilton's mansion; the latter, and the land immediately around it, is now in separate ownership so that visitors to the historic landscape arrive via a 'back door', crossing a new footbridge over the River Mole from the car park.

The building is deliberately simple and straightforward: the budget (at £1,380,000) was quite modest. It abuts an eighteenth-century landscaped mound, positioned to screen the working areas of the estate, which contains the WCs. Other spaces – a shop, office, lecture room and tea room plus kitchen – are aligned off a covered arcade along which visitors pass into the park. Educational facilities are placed in a separate block to the rear. The basic material of the buildings is timber, with an external cladding of untreated oak boards. Natural ventilation, thorough insulation and the application of sunshading where needed reinforce the 'green' credentials of the scheme. This is appropriate architecture for the Georgian landscape: unpretentious, practical but elegant, like the best farm buildings of that era.

The visitor centre at Painshill Park is approached via a footbridge across the River Mole. A very clear diagram arranges shop, meeting-room and café along one side of an open arcade, with education spaces tucked away to the rear. The building is clad in untreated oak intended to weather agreeably.

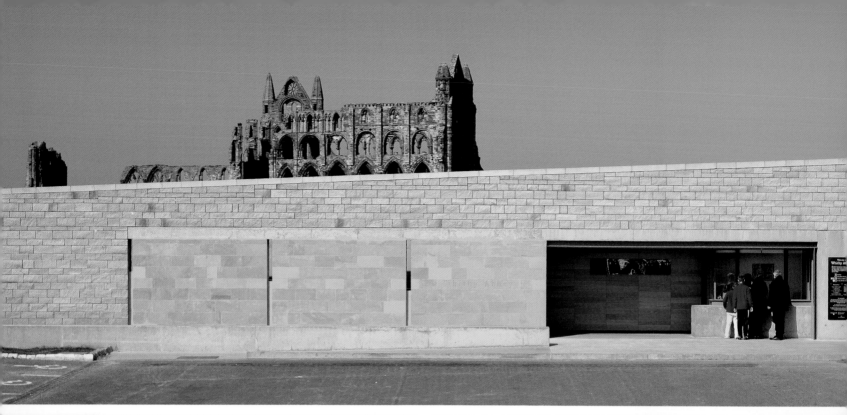

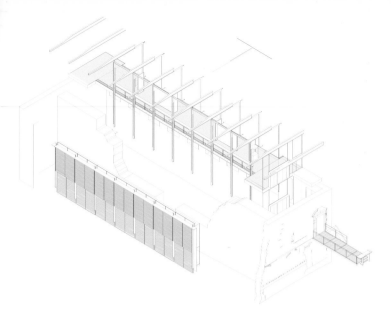

WHITBY ABBEY VISITOR CENTRE AND MUSEUM
WHITBY, NORTH YORKSHIRE

STANTON WILLIAMS, 1998–2002

Stanton Williams is a London practice with a reputation for an almost obsessive interest in detail and the appropriate use of fine materials, and for a sure touch when faced with the problem of adding new elements to historic buildings. It was a natural choice for the Whitby project, which involved not only new facilities for visitors to the medieval abbey (dramatically located on a headland overlooking the North Sea) but also the rationalization of parking and access routes around the site.

Just west of the abbey ruins is the Classical mansion built by Sir Hugh Cholmley in the 1670s and abandoned during the eighteenth century; it survived as a rather melancholy shell, roofless and with its windows blocked up. Stanton Williams's building is a free-standing, two-storey steel-framed structure, with a lightweight zinc-clad roof, sitting within the shell of the old house; it contains a large exhibition space on two levels, plus a shop and ticketing point. (A café is provided elsewhere on the site.) The lightness of the structure minimizes potential damage to buried archaeological remains and makes a minimal impact on

the fabric of the listed house (to which it is lightly tied). The south wall of the Cholmley mansion had largely vanished, so that the elevation of the new building clearly emerges as a curtain of glass screened by timber boarding and steel louvres. On the intact northern elevation the blocked windows have been opened up and filled with plain glass, so that from the inside, despite metal-gauze screening, they offer fine views of the town and sea.

The interior of the building is beautifully made, with new elements in timber, steel and glass contrasting sharply with the rough stone and brickwork of the seventeenth-century house. Display cases, benches and other fittings were designed by the architects. A steel and glass bridge takes visitors from the first floor of the centre directly into the abbey grounds (a considerable part of which was previously inaccessible). Visitors who arrive by car use the southern entrance to the site, where there is another ticketing point. The parking is screened by the natural fall of the land: the cars that had previously littered the headland have been banished.

The entry point to Whitby Abbey from the car park is deliberately understated and set well away from the abbey ruins. The visitor centre itself is constructed on a free-standing steel frame within the shell of the seventeenth-century Cholmley mansion. Inside the building, steel, glass, timber and stone are elegantly used. The rear elevation, largely of glass, is screened by timber boarding and steel louvres, the original wall having collapsed a long time ago.

THE WOMEN'S LIBRARY
WHITECHAPEL, LONDON E1

WRIGHT & WRIGHT ARCHITECTS, 1997–2002

Behind a retained façade inscribed "Wash Houses" – a memory of the old East End of London – the Women's Library is an exquisitely crafted structure in a classic modern tradition. Inside, the emphasis is on careful detail, the controlled use of natural light, and calm and even sober spaces for reading and study.

The Women's Library is not a new institution: the feminist pioneer Millicent Fawcett founded it as long ago as 1926 and it has since evolved as an archive of international importance. The library has belonged to London Guildhall University for a quarter of a century and has finally found a worthy home at the university's Whitechapel campus.

The site is appropriate. The public baths and wash-house that stood there was a place of women's work for more than a century as well as a focus of community life. The 1840s façade, with its inscription "Wash Houses", has been retained as part of the development. Behind it, the new building rises to a total height of six storeys. Apart from a reading room and extensive stacks, the building contains exhibition and seminar spaces, meeting-rooms and a café. The entrance area is a dramatic double-height space, with exhibition areas surrounding a hexagonal lecture theatre, opening on to a garden court on the north side of the building. The exhibition space can accommodate large exhibits – suffragette banners, for example – or act as a break-out area from the lecture room. There is a café at first-floor level behind the arched windows in the retained façade.

This is a carefully crafted building in the Cambridge-rooted modern tradition, which generated, *inter alia*, Colin St John Wilson and Allies & Morrison. Soft red brick, stone, oak and smooth plaster are used internally to create a rich and calm ambience – "an exquisitely crafted casket", as critic Catherine Slessor called it – yet the interior does not lack spatial drama. The solidity of the architecture reflects a serious commitment to energy-saving: heavy insulation and passive cooling devices remove the need for mechanical ventilation, even in archive storage areas. The art programme for the building is ambitious. This is a beautifully wrought, thoughtful and sober building that eschews fashion to make its point: one feels that the leaders of the suffragette movement would have loved it. It is a fine addition to the fabric of the East End.

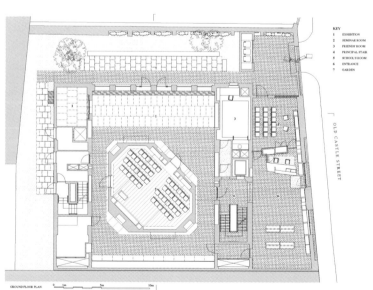

GROUND FLOOR PLAN

KEY
1 EXHIBITION
2 SEMINAR ROOM
3 FRIENDS' ROOM
4 PRINCIPAL STAIR
5 SCHOOL'S ROOM
6 ENTRANCE
7 GARDEN

OLD CASTLE STREET

The interventions made to the listed barn at Wycoller are deliberately demountable and essentially temporary, with no lasting impact on the historic fabric. The use of the building as a facility for walkers has been extended to make the building a resource for the local community. This is an interesting and original approach to the reuse of a building type that is fundamental to the character of the British countryside.

WYCOLLER VISITOR CENTRE
NR COLNE, LANCASHIRE
HAKES ASSOCIATES, 2000–02

Barns remain a common feature of the British countryside, although fewer and fewer are put to agricultural use. The most popular alternative use is residential, but the results are rarely satisfactory: the compartmented clutter of modern lifestyles destroys what were once magnificent open spaces, while former farmyards are converted into car parks or prettified suburban gardens.

The sixteenth-century aisled barn at Wycoller village, near Colne, has long been used as an informal facility for walkers on the Pendle Way and Brontë Trail, and for school parties pursuing projects in the area. The decision to refurbish the building and extend its use reflected the drive to diversify the rural economy and create new sources of employment. The aim was to provide an enclosed information centre, open for only part of the year. The remainder of the space was to be freely open at all times, but improvements were needed to make it usable for a range of local acitivities and to facilitate access.

Hakes Associates' approach was to preserve the great internal space of the barn uncompromised, by respecting the historic fabric and making any new intervention a demountable object clearly detached from the listed building. The project was achieved to a tight schedule – a construction phase of six weeks – and at a cost of just £120,000.

The new stage, visitor kiosk and information wall are concentrated into one area of the internal space, which is left open for use as a performance and teaching area, and mounted on adjustable legs to cope with an uneven floor. These elements were fabricated off-site and delivered as a kit of parts for assembly. A ramped approach to the stage area allows full disabled access. As part of the scheme, a repair programme was carried out on the barn using traditional techniques.

This project, by a young practice, has spontaneity, verve and sensitivity, and the barn has emerged clearly as a local community amenity.

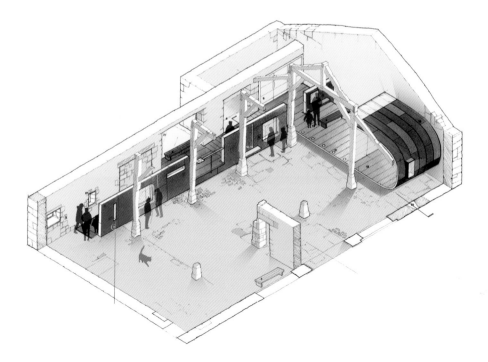

YORKSHIRE SCULPTURE PARK VISITOR CENTRE
WAKEFIELD, WEST YORKSHIRE

FEILDEN CLEGG BRADLEY, 1995–2002

The Yorkshire Sculpture Park (YSP) at Wakefield, West Yorkshire, is a remarkable institution that exhibits large-scale works of sculpture in the Georgian landscape park around Bretton Hall near by (itself used for many years as a college). Feilden Clegg Bradley has worked for the YSP for many years, designing a demountable fabric structure to act as a covered gallery and adapting a derelict gardener's bothy as additional display space. The visitor centre is the centrepiece of a development plan for the site that has rationalized access routes and car parking, acknowledging that the sculpture park is now a potent and permanent presence there. A new entrance into the site follows the line of the 1801 park entrance from the main road, thus removing visitor traffic from Bretton village. The visitor centre is placed close to the new entrance, at the point (marked by a ha-ha) where the formal gardens around the hall meet the more informal deer park beyond, and on an established axis defined by the terrace dividing the formal gardens from the kitchen gardens.

The diagram of the visitor building is closely related to that of the same practice's visitor facilities at Painshill Park, Surrey (see p. 81), but on a larger scale. Two storeys of accommodation – shop, café, meeting-rooms, education spaces and WCs – are arranged along a linear concourse that is also used as a gallery space. Areas not requiring natural light are buried into the rising ground to the north. The shop and café are in a lightweight timber and glass pavilion south of the concourse, with fine views over the landscape.

Feilden Clegg Bradley has long been associated with an environmentally friendly approach. The building is designed for low-energy operation, making optimum use of daylight, natural ventilation and the insulating effects of thermal mass. Likewise, the choice of materials was, it is claimed, equally influenced by environmental considerations: the stone used in the concourse floor and spine wall is from the Pennines, not a costly import. (The architects wanted to use local oak for the cladding, but it proved too expensive; red cedar from a sustainable source was imported from Canada instead.) The mix of stone, timber and render is, however, used with elegance and wit.

Feilden Clegg Bradley may be environmentally sound (so much so that it is designing the new headquarters for the National Trust), but it is not a hair-shirt operation. The new gallery designed by the same architects for a site beneath the lawns of the Bothy Garden at Bretton, on axis with the visitor centre, is eagerly awaited.

The visitor centre stands on a site that boasts spectacular views over the park at Bretton and the surrounding countryside. The building marks the transition point from the formal gardens around Bretton Hall to the extensive deer park beyond. The diagram places two storeys of accommodation along a linear concourse.

ASCOT RACECOURSE DEVELOPMENT, ASCOT, BERKSHIRE
HOK SPORT

**BANDSTAND, DE LA WARR PAVILION, BEXHILL-ON-SEA
EAST SUSSEX**
NIALL McLAUGHLIN ARCHITECTS

BARBICAN CENTRE REFURBISHMENT, LONDON EC2
ALLFORD HALL MONAGHAN MORRIS

c/PLEX, WEST BROMWICH, WEST MIDLANDS
ALSOP ARCHITECTS

CITY OF MANCHESTER STADIUM, MANCHESTER
ARUP ASSOCIATES

**DRUMKINNON TOWER VISITOR ATTRACTION, LOCH LOMOND
DUMBARTONSHIRE**
PAGE & PARK ARCHITECTS

**GATEWAY AND ORIENTATION CENTRE, LOCH LOMOND
DUMBARTONSHIRE**
BENNETTS ASSOCIATES

HAMPSTEAD THEATRE, SWISS COTTAGE, LONDON NW3
BENNETTS ASSOCIATES

**LEICESTER THEATRE AND PERFORMING ARTS CENTRE
LEICESTER**
RAFAEL VIÑOLY ARCHITECTS

**MAGNA SCIENCE ADVENTURE CENTRE, ROTHERHAM
SOUTH YORKSHIRE**
WILKINSON EYRE ARCHITECTS

**THE MARKET PLACE THEATRE AND ARTS CENTRE, ARMAGH
COUNTY ARMAGH**
GLENN HOWELLS ARCHITECTS

THE SAGE, GATESHEAD, TYNE AND WEAR
FOSTER AND PARTNERS

TOLBOOTH ARTS CENTRE, STIRLING, STIRLINGSHIRE
RICHARD MURPHY ARCHITECTS/SIMPSON & BROWN ARCHITECTS

WALES MILLENNIUM CENTRE, CARDIFF
PERCY THOMAS PARTNERSHIP

**WOLVERHAMPTON CIVIC HALLS, WOLVERHAMPTON
WEST MIDLANDS**
PENOYRE & PRASAD

ASCOT RACECOURSE REDEVELOPMENT
ASCOT, BERKSHIRE

HOK SPORT, 2001–07

Ascot is one of the famous shrines of the international horse-racing circuit, with Royal Ascot a major event of the social season every summer. It is an unlikely location for radical new design. Yet HOK Sport's £180,000,000, five-year project is set to transform Ascot (the property of the Crown): other courses have added new facilities but it has opted for virtually total redevelopment. The existing 1960s grandstand will be demolished, the parade ring relocated and the track itself, with its famous 'Straight Mile', realigned to provide space for new development. Work on the course itself started in 2002.

The new stand, scheduled for construction in 2004–07, is the focal point

of the scheme. The aim is to create a world-class building in which spectator comfort and safety are the primary concerns, but the issue of funding the sport is also addressed. There will be 280 private boxes for corporate entertaining and a 200-bed luxury hotel, with rooms overlooking the course. The great central galleria of the stand will provide access to the seating and to high-quality restaurants and bars available to all racegoers: racing's traditional élitism is seen as increasingly outdated, and year-round use for conferences and banqueting is becoming the norm. The stand is a strikingly light and airy structure, designed in association with engineers Buro Happold and topped with a

Teflon-coated glass-fibre roof. The galleria is naturally ventilated, using large opening louvres, and unheated. The new parade ring is covered and easily accessible from the stand. According to Rod Sheard of HOK Sport, "the aim is to banish the seediness which many associate with racing; people will pay for quality".

The overall capacity of the course (80,000) will not be increased, but the construction of a new underground service route will reduce traffic through the town of Ascot. Racing at Ascot began in the reign of Queen Anne, in the early eighteenth century; this project propels a great British institution into the high-tech, high-finance world of global sport and events.

The focal point of the redevelopment of the racecourse at Ascot is the new stand with its central galleria, daylit, naturally ventillated and providing access to the seating areas and private boxes. Massive in scale, the project incorporates a 200-bed luxury hotel.

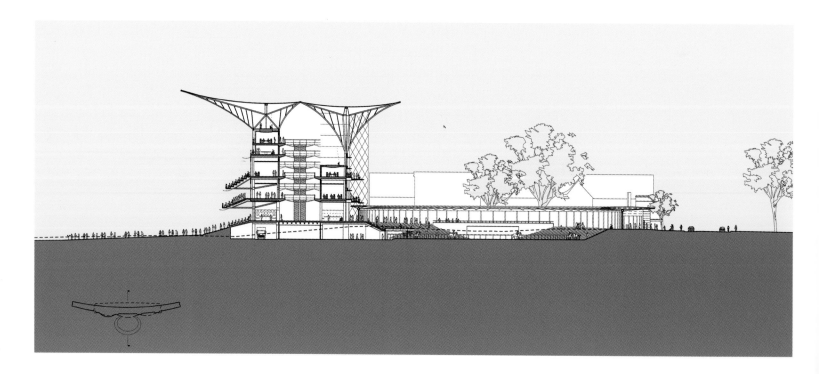

BANDSTAND, DE LA WARR PAVILION
BEXHILL-ON-SEA, EAST SUSSEX
NIALL McLAUGHLIN ARCHITECTS, 2001

Bexhill's De La Warr Pavilion, designed by Erich Mendelsohn and Serge Chermayeff and opened in 1935, is one of Britain's most notable Modern Movement monuments. After years of uncertainty the building is the subject of a major restoration and upgrading project, with John McAslan & Partners as architects.

Niall McLaughlin's bandstand, which cost just £54,000, is a symbol of the renewed vitality of the pavilion and, it is hoped, its bright future, but also harks back to the seaside tradition of open-air entertainment. Working with engineers Price & Myers, McLaughlin produced a

design that is innovative in form and materials. The structure – is it a building or a large piece of furniture? – is of fibreglass on a timber-and-steel frame, the steel giving the structure the necessary weight to withstand English Channel gales. Wheels allow the bandstand to be moved around the site.

Though not a practical bandstand in the conventional sense of the term – it provides minimum cover for very few people on a wet day – this project is both evocative and optimistic. Its symbolic nature, and the verve with which it was designed, are what count.

Niall McLaughlin's bandstand is more significant, perhaps, for its symbolism evoking the traditional spirit of the seaside than for its practical utility as a shelter for musicians. Nevertheless, it is a lively response to the De La Warr Pavilion, which remains a much-loved icon of the British Modern Movement.

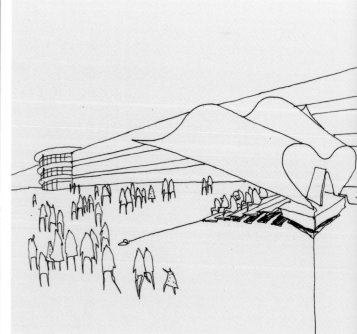

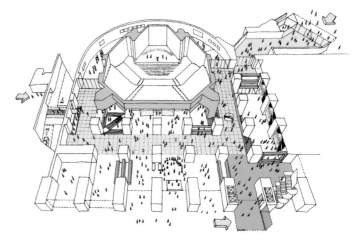

BARBICAN CENTRE REFURBISHMENT LONDON EC2

ALLFORD HALL MONAGHAN MORRIS, 2000–06

The Barbican is one of the heroic achievements of modern architecture in Britain. The first ideas for the dense, high-rise development, on 14 hectares (35 acres) of bomb-devastated land on the northern edge of the City, were produced by the practice Chamberlin, Powell & Bon as early as 1955. The scheme, containing over 2000 flats, was completed only with the opening of the arts centre in 1982. By that date the project seemed inevitably out of tune with the times, but its qualities are now widely appreciated: the entire Barbican was listed Grade II in 2001.

The masterplan by Allford Hall Monaghan Morris (AHMM) for the arts centre was already under development at that time, the practice having been commissioned to produce it in 2000. During 2001 a skilful and sympathetic refurbishment of the Barbican concert hall (by Caruso St John, working with acousticians Kirkegaard Associates) was completed.

AHMM's scheme, programmed for phased construction in 2003–06, seeks to tackle some of the practical problems inherent in the original concept for the centre, for example the perceived illegibility of the building and the lack of clear routes to the various facilities it contains (including two theatres, a concert hall, galleries, cinemas, a library, conference and exhibition spaces, restaurants and bars). It also aims to repair the damage done by random, largely cosmetic changes to the building during the 1990s, when its architecture was still unfashionable.

The centre has always lacked, albeit deliberately, a main entrance: visitors can arrive on different levels and often feel disorientated. A key element in the proposals is the creation of two clearly marked principal points of arrival: from Silk Street (where the Barbican meets the rest of the City) and at the Lakeside, the internal focus of the complex. A new bridge, 7.5 metres (25 feet) wide, connects the two entrances, forming a bold, if controversial, intervention into the main foyer space. The existing 1990s bridge, a feeble and utterly inappropriate intrusion, is to be removed, opening to view the façade of the main theatre. Central to the project is the reinstatement of the 'buildings-within-a-building' idea inherent in the original designs. Colour coding and new signage are designed to help users navigate their way around the centre. Bars, cafés and box offices are to be rationalized and relocated: the existing, gloomy ground-level bar, for example, will be resited close to the lakeside terrace. Major changes are also planned to the Barbican Art Gallery, which has never worked well, thanks partly to late changes to the original brief.

The changes are substantial, but the Barbican Centre is tough enough to withstand them. Given AHMM's record of sympathetic reworking of modern classics – for example the Monsoon Building in Paddington, west London – there is every reason to hope that the practice will unlock some of the centre's unrealized potential without undermining its essential character.

It has long been argued that, whatever its virtues, the Barbican is a difficult place in which to find one's way around. The refurbishment project aims to address this problem, and also to banish some of the ill-advised and essentially cosmetic additions of the 1980s and 1990s. The principal new interventions are the establishment of clearer entrance points and a new bridge linking parts of the massive foyer.

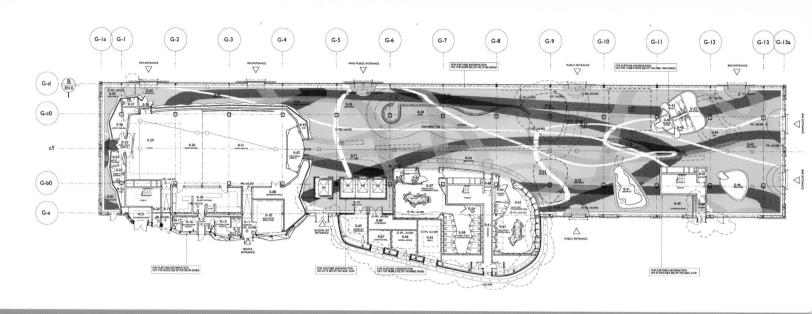

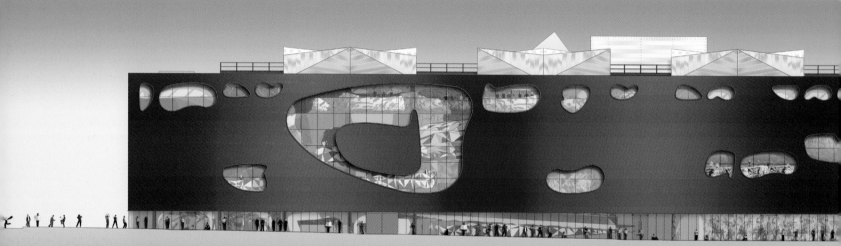

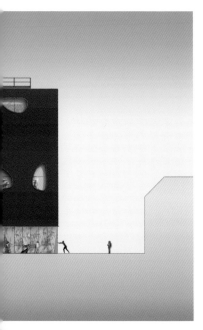

c/PLEX, WEST BROMWICH, WEST MIDLANDS
ALSOP ARCHITECTS, 1998–2004

Some of the key projects in Will Alsop's earlier career – the Pompidou Centre, Paris, for which he submitted a remarkable competition scheme while still a student; InterAction in Kentish Town, north London, on which he worked for Cedric Price; and Riverside Studios in Hammersmith, west London, for which he drew up an ambitious, if abortive, development scheme – reflect a dynamic view of the arts and society. Working with communities has been one of his preoccupations over many years, so he was a natural choice, in 1998, for the c/PLEX project in West Bromwich, a former market and industrial town north-west of central Birmingham.

The idea of c/PLEX had emerged from Jubilee Arts, a body with twenty-five years' experience in promoting community arts activities in the town. The development was to contain not only a theatre, cinema and gallery, but also studios and spaces for artists and major provision for education and public participation. The agenda for the project was unashamedly regenerative. West Bromwich was perceived as a small town (population 50,000) with no distinctive identity or image. Its central area, poorly developed in the post-war period, was in decline. As the new art gallery in nearby Walsall was to prove, however, investment in 'cultural industries' can turn around the image of a place.

At c/PLEX, for which the site was a dismal 1960s bus station on the edge of the town centre, Alsop developed ideas that had emerged in his unbuilt Swansea Literature Centre and the award-winning Peckham Library in south London. The first version of the scheme saw the building elevated above a sheltered public square – a beacon of culture visible from the nearby M5 motorway. The various art spaces were to be contained within a translucent envelope on which works of art, texts or messages could be projected. In the built version (for which Lottery funding was finally secured in 2002), the centre has "come down to ground", without the covered square. The radical ideas and forms, however, remain. c/PLEX will be Alsop's largest building in Britain to date and a key marker in his quest for a place at the very summit of the British architectural scene.

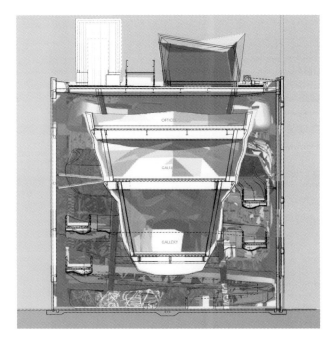

Will Alsop's c/PLEX, a project that uses the arts as a catalyst for urban regeneration, takes the form of a dramatic and colourful container in which performance, gallery, studio and education spaces are disposed around public circulation routes, encouraging participation in the activities it houses.

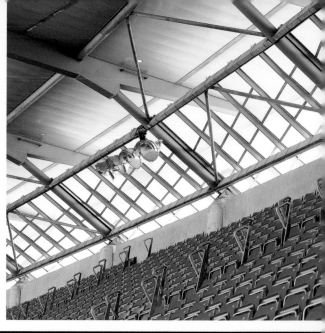

CITY OF MANCHESTER STADIUM, MANCHESTER
ARUP ASSOCIATES, 1995–2003

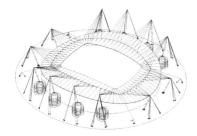

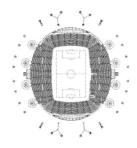

While the future of Wembley Stadium in London languished in limbo – work finally got under way in the late summer of 2002 – the city of Manchester built a £110,000,000, 41,000-seat, state-of-the-art venue that has been adapted for use from athletics to football. The project was fast-tracked by the decision to hold the Commonwealth Games in Manchester in 2002. This was in itself something of a consolation prize. In the early 1990s the city had bid to host the 2000 Olympic Games (for which Sydney was chosen), bringing in Arup to produce designs for an 80,000-seat stadium. In 1995 Manchester put forward the same site for the proposed National Stadium, but the prize went to London. This site, far from the revitalized city centre in the bleak wastelands of east Manchester (which are currently the focus of a massive regeneration campaign), was finally developed for the Commonwealth Games. Other facilities developed for the 2002

event, including a velodrome and sports institute, are clustered near by. After the closure of the games the stadium was adapted for permanent use by Manchester City Football Club.

The Arup team was a close integration of architects and engineers. The aim was clearly to create a landmark: the great masts that carry the roof are visible from far away across the flat Mancunian landscape. Massive circulation ramps form two groups of drums along the eastern and western sides of the stadium, and the bases for eight of the twelve masts. The cable-net roof carries lightweight polycarbonate and aluminium roof cladding. The form of the roof is both extremely elegant and highly cost-efficient, and was the result of close architect–engineer dialogue. The use of a traditional construction management contract rather than a design-and-build approach was far more than a technicality: it probably ensured the quality of detail that

sets this stadium apart from some other recently developed sports facilities in Britain. The architecture of sport is increasingly part of the mainstream of design, yet the sheer complexity of the task of creating it makes it, ironically, a sophisticated speciality where only the big players – Arup, HOK, Foster – can effectively compete.

The adaptation of the stadium for football matches allowed its capacity to be increased to 48,500. With the central area excavated a further 6 metres (20 feet) for the new pitch, the athletics track removed and the seating reconfigured, the completion of the roof over the north stand made the stadium into a completely enclosed bowl. It remains to be seen whether the move to a new home (in August 2003) will restore Manchester City's fortunes. For east Manchester, however, the stadium is a truly remarkable gesture of confidence.

Opposite
The City of Manchester Stadium is a landmark in the wastelands of east Manchester – now earmarked for a major regeneration programme.

Above and right
The roof structure is not only striking but also highly economical. It was extended when the stadium was adapted, after the end of the Commonwealth Games in 2002, to house Manchester City Football Club.

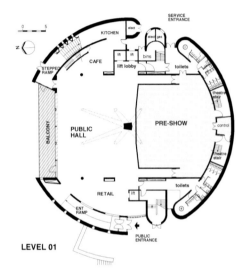

CROSS SECTION TO EAST

VIEWING GALLERY · PROJECTION · FILM THEATRE · STEPPED RAMP · PUBLIC HALL · PRE-SHOW · THEATRE ST AIR

LEVEL 01

STEPPED RAMP · KITCHEN · SERVICE ENTRANCE · elect · elect gas · bins · CAFE · lift · lift · lift lobby · toilets · BALCONY · PUBLIC HALL · PRE-SHOW · control · theatre stair · RETAIL · theatre stair · toilets · ENT RAMP · lift · PUBLIC ENTRANCE

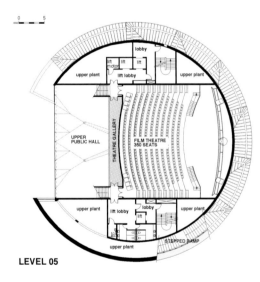

LEVEL 05

lobby · upper plant · lift · lift · lift · lift motor · lift lobby · upper plant · UPPER PUBLIC HALL · THEATRE GALLERY · FILM THEATRE 350 SEATS · upper plant · upper plant · lobby · lift lobby · lift · upper plant · upper plant · STEPPED RAMP

DRUMKINNON TOWER VISITOR ATTRACTION
LOCH LOMOND, DUMBARTONSHIRE
PAGE & PARK ARCHITECTS, 1999–2002

Advance publicity for the visitor attraction building at Loch Lomond, describing it as "a modern-day castle built in traditional Scottish style", and subsequent critical comment ("Disney-like", declared one journalist) were not calculated to please the architects. The Glasgow-based practice Page & Park is known for its highly individual design philosophy and its far from superficial interest in history: its Italian Centre, for example, remains one of the best recent developments in central Glasgow.

The challenge for Page & Park when it won the commission in 1999 was to produce a substantial, sturdy building, to a tight budget, that extended the visitor's experience of a visit to Loch Lomond: "a building to be explored and experienced and interpreted in one's own way." There was no attempt by the architects to design a "modern-day castle"; references to Scottish traditions are oblique and abstracted, rather than literal.

Loch Lomond was included in Scotland's first National Park, officially designated in 2002. Half a century earlier Patrick Abercrombie had described the southern end of the loch as "a disgraceful introduction to such a wonderland of natural beauty". Page & Park's building, along with the orientation centre designed by Bennetts Associates (see pp. 104–05) and the associated retail development, were intended to provide the reception point that Abercrombie had called for. The client was a consortium of local authorities, and the agenda one of regeneration and job creation.

The fit-out of Drumkinnon Tower, as Page & Park's building was subsequently named, was always intended to be commercially driven, with a 350-seat I-Werks cinema, shops and café as part of the visitor experience, which culminates in a spectacular view of loch and mountains from the roof-top terrace. The circular form of the building as a whole reflects the drum shape of the cinema. The pressure to maximize retail space has reduced the quality of the interior, but Page & Park's granite shell, juxtaposed with a sheer wall of glazing, remains impressive, as does the use of exposed concrete inside the building. For some Scottish critics Drumkinnon Tower represents a retreat into a false Scottishness at a time when Scotland should be looking outwards rather than picking over its own past. The fusion of modernity and tradition in the building is, in fact, oddly reminiscent of the work of a leading Scottish architect of an earlier generation, Basil Spence.

Opposite
Drumkinnon Tower forms part of a complex of visitor facilities on the shore of Loch Lomond. Whilst the building clearly makes reference to the Scottish building tradition, its interiors are anything but historicist.

Left
The greater part of the building is occupied by a 350-seat film theatre, with a viewing gallery at roof level.

GATEWAY AND ORIENTATION CENTRE
LOCH LOMOND, DUMBARTONSHIRE

BENNETTS ASSOCIATES, 1999–2002

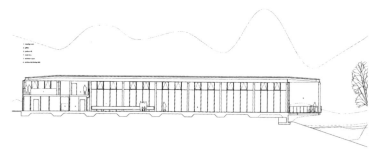

Like Page & Park's visitor attraction (see pp. 102–03), Bennetts Associates' Gateway building at Loch Lomond was a spin-off from the decision to designate Loch Lomond and the surrounding area of the Trossachs as Scotland's first national park. Already a major tourist destination and a 'lung' for Scotland's two large conurbations, the area is expected to attract more than one million visitors annually. Both the Page & Park and Bennetts Associates projects, and the associated retail development and parking area, form components in a masterplan by Ian White Associates.

Bennetts Associates was commissioned by a coalition of local authorities and public agencies in 1999 to provide a reception and orientation centre, with exhibition space, shop and offices. In contrast to Page & Park's building, with its pronounced references to the historic architecture of Scotland, Bennetts' Gateway is a steel and glass pavilion, frankly inspired by Mies van der Rohe, which would not be out of place in an American national park. Sitting close to the water's edge, with a fine belt of trees as its backdrop, the rectangular building (54 x 12 metres/177 x 40 feet) contains a

double-height exhibition space, with a viewing platform cantilevering out over the loch, and a two-storey administration area. Structurally, it is straightforward: a series of portal frames containing a fully glazed façade. The exact and elegant detailing, very much in the Miesian tradition, lifts the building beyond the purely functional. An oak ceiling and a floor of local stone help root the Gateway to its setting.

Along its south elevation the building is set behind a screen 100 metres (328 feet) long formed of green oak; the timber was a gift from the French national parks authority and was sourced from trees blown down in the disastrous storm of 1999. The visitor entrance lobby and office staircase are allowed to emerge proud of the screen, which is seen as "a threshold between the adjacent man-made environment and the natural landscape of the promontory". Like Munkenbeck & Marshall's Isle of Bute visitor centre (see pp. 72–73), this building eschews 'Scottishness'. Although Rab Bennetts is a Scot, perhaps only architects based outside Scotland can avoid the creeping influence of the vernacular.

Right
Bennetts Associates' Gateway building at Loch Lomond takes its inspiration from the work of Mies van der Rohe and is international, rather than specifically Scottish, in flavour.

Opposite
The building sits happily in a magnificent natural setting. A long screen of green oak ties it to its immediate woodland context.

HAMPSTEAD THEATRE
SWISS COTTAGE, LONDON NW3

BENNETTS ASSOCIATES, 1994–2003

The new Hampstead Theatre is the first entirely new theatre built in London since the completion of Denys Lasdun's National Theatre, on the South Bank, in 1975. It provides a well-equipped permanent home for an institution that has built up a striking artistic reputation over nearly forty years despite using distinctly makeshift premises.

By the 1990s the extended Portakabin, next to the Swiss Cottage Baths and Library, that served as Hampstead Theatre was in a poor state. Bennetts Associates was commissioned as early as 1994 to work on plans for a new theatre, initially on the same site, but it soon became clear that there were advantages in relocating it to the north, close to Eton Avenue, where it would replace an unsightly block of public conveniences. Bennetts subsequently produced a masterplan for the entire site, in line with Camden Council's aim to regenerate the area. In the 1960s Basil

Spence had proposed a new town hall for Camden at Swiss Cottage, alongside the baths and library, but it was never realized. Much of the site therefore remained unresolved and rather unpleasant left-over open space, shut off from the street. The baths have now been demolished, while the library, a listed building, is being refurbished by John McAslan. New leisure facilities are being developed, together with housing, to a concept by Terry Farrell. The landscape plan for the site has been developed by Gustafson Porter.

The new theatre, finally built in 2000–03 with the aid of Arts Lottery funding, contains a single elliptical auditorium, with flexible seating for up to 330 people, that aims to retain the sense of intimacy that was the great strength of the old theatre while doubling seating capacity. The stage, adaptable for proscenium or open-plan productions, and workshop facilities are

vastly improved, as are the dressing-rooms and offices; there is also a dedicated rehearsal space and education room (which can be used as a small studio theatre).

The main entrance is directly from Eton Avenue. Once inside, it becomes apparent to the visitor that the building has three storeys, two above ground and one below. Bridges and ramps channel audiences into the auditorium. Mechanical services are concentrated at basement level in a space that extends below the adjacent landscaped park. The aim was to provide access to the building at street level, removing the need for ramps or lifts. Achieving this meant securing consent from other building owners to move the car-park ramp serving an adjacent office block: it now runs through the theatre basement.

The auditorium reads as a strongly modelled solid mass, clad in matt zinc, clearly rising through the largely transparent

pavilion (in which areas of timber slatting punctuate the glazing), which contains the foyers and other public spaces. Finishes in the foyer areas are simple and durable – steel, concrete and timber – with lighting devised by Martin Richman dramatizing the space. The auditorium is lined in timber, with colour adding warmth and texture. The architects cite the rustic Georgian theatre at Richmond, North Yorkshire, as an exemplar for the comfortable but informal ambience they have sought to create.

Bennetts Associates had no experience of theatre design when it tackled this project, and perhaps this was an advantage. The building reflects close collaboration between client and architect. It remains to be seen what impact the move to new premises will have on the famously innovative Hampstead Theatre, but Swiss Cottage has certainly gained an impressive new public landmark.

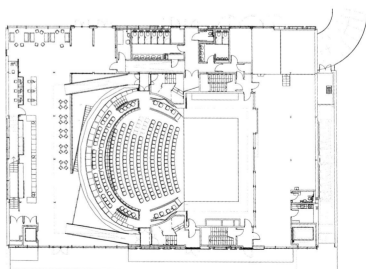

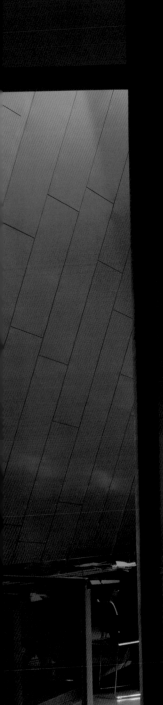

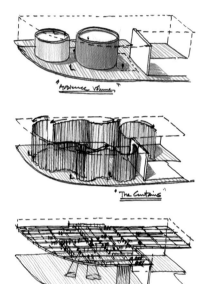

Leicester compares badly with other British cities in terms of its theatrical provision. Nottingham has its Playhouse and Sheffield, The Crucible, and both also have fine Victorian theatres. Leicester (where the Theatre Royal was demolished in 1958) has only the Haymarket, stranded on top of a 1960s shopping centre, and the Phoenix, a lively institution but housed in premises always regarded as temporary.

The new Theatre and Performing Arts Centre, the first major project undertaken in Britain by the leading New York practice Rafael Viñoly Architects, forms part of an intended cultural quarter around Rutland Street and St George's Church, an 1820s structure no longer required for worship but with potential for reuse. The former Odeon Cinema stands across Rutland Street from the theatre site and could be revitalized as

another arts venue. The site of the theatre has long been used as a car park, with a large multi-storey car park adjacent, but includes a listed warehouse that is to be retained. The cultural quarter is part of an overall vision for regenerating the city centre as a focus of activity and employment.

Having won a limited competition in 2002, the architects have worked with the local authority to develop the programme for a dynamic new arts centre. The aim was to create a theatre open to the city, even to the extent of exposing its inner workings to the street. Two theatre auditoria are proposed, seating 750 and 350 respectively, the smaller intended to have an experimental workshop ethos.

The architectural strategy is to place the performance spaces as free-standing

containers within an open enclosure, a public space that forms a level extension of the street. The aim is to break down the divide between front- and back-of-house, between foyer and performance space, and to provide for maximum flexibility of use. Moveable partitions allow the main stage to be reconfigured as required for both theatres. The container itself is a strikingly transparent structure along its street elevations. Storage and dressing-room spaces are disposed along the northern and western edges of the site, where it is enclosed by buildings. Instead of being hidden behind closed doors, actors will cross the foyer *en route* to the stage. Theatre is a total experience, say the architects, in which everyone participates. This building reflects that idea.

Above
The diagram of the theatre places two auditoria within the glazed box that contains the foyer and circulation spaces, which are clearly visible from the street.

Opposite and right
The theatre is a powerful, even dominant presence in a new 'cultural quarter'. Existing buildings of value are retained in the scheme.

MAGNA SCIENCE ADVENTURE CENTRE
ROTHERHAM, SOUTH YORKSHIRE

WILKINSON EYRE ARCHITECTS, 1998–2001

The Magna Science Adventure Centre, opened in summer 2001, was one of the last major projects funded by the Millennium Commission from Lottery funds. In contrast to other Millennium schemes, involving new landmark buildings, Magna is essentially a conversion, if one on a grand scale. This did not stop it winning the RIBA's coveted Stirling Prize in 2001, from a shortlist that included Nicholas Grimshaw's Eden Project in Cornwall (see pp. 58–59). It has since proved a remarkably successful tourist attraction and runs an ambitious education programme.

The 'raw material' for Magna was the former Templeborough Melting Shop, a huge steelworks (it once employed 10,000 men) that opened in 1917. Its closure in 1993 was part of a carnage of the region's heavy industries – steel and coal – that reached its peak during the era in which

Margaret Thatcher was prime minister and resulted in high levels of unemployment. There was strong local interest in retaining the works as a monument to the steel industry and its workforce. Initially a steel heritage centre was the objective. After Wilkinson Eyre was brought in during 1998 the emphasis changed, in line with the educational and regenerative agenda of the National Lottery.

The container for Magna is a double-aisled, steel-framed shed, 350 metres (1150 feet) long and with an internal height of 30 metres (100 feet). Within this huge volume (which remains an 'inside/outside' space, without mechanical servicing) much of the original machinery, and with it the ethos of steel-making, has been left as found. A massive crane rail extending the length of the shed was capable of supporting enormous loadings.

The container has enormous potential for future development and change. At present the ground floor remains largely empty. Visitors are safely channelled along an upper-level walkway that accesses four pavilions themed on the four elements of air, earth, water and fire. The water and air pavilions are lightweight ovoid structures, finely engineered, as one would expect from a practice with its roots in High-tech architecture, but also surprisingly expressive in form. The success of Magna is, however, not entirely architectural. For all its serious intentions it is a well-conceived piece of theatre, generated by dramatic lighting, fire, sparks and bangs: all the thrills of heavy industry without the sweat or risks. It is, of course, all too easy to be cynical about a project of this kind, but it has rekindled local pride and attracted visitors and money to an area that badly needed a boost.

Above and below
The Magna project combines the reuse of a durable historic structure – the huge steel shed of a former steelworks – with shapely and memorable new forms.

Opposite
New interventions float freely in the vast internal space.

WATER

THE MARKET PLACE THEATRE AND ARTS CENTRE
ARMAGH, COUNTY ARMAGH

GLENN HOWELLS ARCHITECTS, 1996–2001

With its two cathedrals, Armagh is the spiritual capital of all Ireland for both Roman Catholics and Protestants, a fact that did not protect the city from the activities of terrorists. In the 1980s a bomb destroyed the city's arts centre; Glenn Howells was appointed to design its replacement after a competition held in 1996. Completed in 2001, The Market Place reinforced Birmingham-based Howells' position as a leading player on the national architectural scene.

The site is close to, and slopes steeply away from, the ancient Anglican cathedral at the heart of Armagh. The brief provided for a theatre seating 400, a smaller studio theatre, an art gallery, artists' studios and workshops, and bars and a restaurant. The issue of context was inevitably critical in the design of the project. Howells avoided, however, any concessions to historicism or quaintness. His building has a simple but satisfying dignity of its own: cast-stone cladding, similar in hue to the characteristic local limestone, is used on all exteriors.

The building consists of a series of connected top-lit spaces, enclosed by massive walls that ensure acoustic insulation and are a vital ingredient of a low-energy services strategy. The main theatre, with its projecting fly tower, is placed at the bottom of the slope, to reduce its visual impact on views of the cathedral. An internal route connects all the spaces. The foyer runs parallel, along the square, gradually increasing in height down the slope.

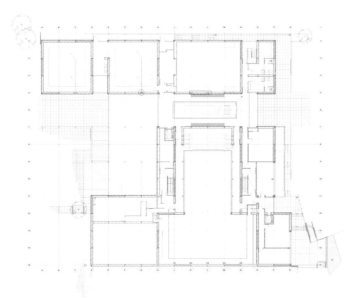

Above and left
The Market Place, containing two theatres, a gallery, studios and other amenities, respects the scale of its context but is uncompromising in its modernity.

Opposite
The use of toplighting is part of a strategy for low-energy running: controlled natural light pervades the principal spaces.

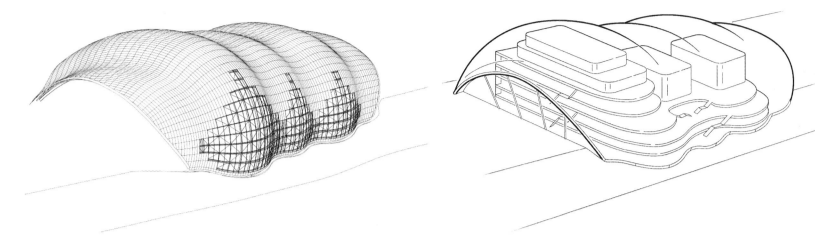

THE SAGE, GATESHEAD
TYNE AND WEAR
FOSTER AND PARTNERS, 1997–2004

Foster's music centre, enigmatically named The Sage, is the third key component in Gateshead's campaign to regenerate its riverside, effectively as an extension of Newcastle's already lively quayside, just across the River Tyne. With the BALTIC arts centre (see pp. 44–45) and Millennium Bridge (see pp. 28–29) already in place, the £70,000,000 building will, it is claimed, cement Gateshead's appeal as an 'arts destination'.

Foster and Partners was commissioned to design the building in 1997, following some years of discussion and planning. The building reflects the practice's interest, developed from the late 1990s, in strong and markedly organic form. Nothing could be further removed from the classical restraint and refinement of the Foster and Partners' Carré d'Art in Nîmes, southern France, than this billowing cloud of a building, but then the windswept and still bleak southern bank of the Tyne lacks the civic traditions of the Mediterranean. Externally the building will be an eye-catcher, while the internal layout reflects the fashionably inclusive agenda of the project. The building will host pop, folk, jazz and classical concerts, and will be the base for the Northern Sinfonia Orchestra and the Folkworks organization, as well as housing a music school open to all. Up to 600,000 visitors are expected annually. The largest of the three auditoria seats 1650, the second, more informal, seats 400, while a rehearsal hall doubles up as an education space. These are surrounded by a very large multi-level public space, containing bars, cafés and shops and intended to encourage intercommunication between performers and audiences. The architect compares the enveloping skin – there is no real distinction between walls and roof – to a 'shrink-wrapping' around the performance spaces. Views out to the river and the Newcastle skyline will be impressive.

The project reflects Foster's successful pursuit of new and freer forms, as well as his remarkable ability to create buildings that cannot be ignored. Whether the hyperbole about The Sage creates the inclusive learning experience that its promoters anticipate is anyone's guess. But the building itself will certainly make waves.

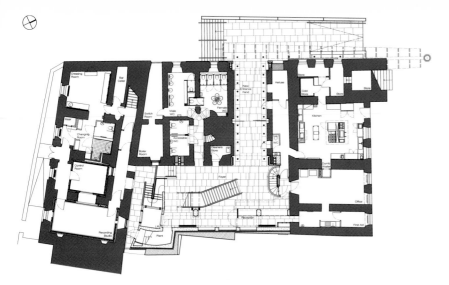

0 1 2 3 4 5 6 7 8 9 10m
Scale

TOLBOOTH ARTS CENTRE, STIRLING
STIRLINGSHIRE

RICHARD MURPHY ARCHITECTS/
SIMPSON & BROWN ARCHITECTS, 1997–2002

English-born Richard Murphy, although already a major star in the Scottish architectural firmament, completed his first large-scale work, the Dundee Contemporary Arts Centre, only in 1999. The context for this project in Stirling, the competition for which Murphy won in 1997, was very different: a Category A-listed historic building in the upper town, close to the famous castle – and resulted in a collaboration with the specialist Edinburgh conservation practice of Simpson & Brown, under the close supervision of Historic Scotland.

The Tolbooth, its steeple a landmark on the skyline of Stirling, was a combination of town hall, law court and prison constructed in phases, around an enclosed courtyard, between 1705 and 1811. The competition brief was to convert the then redundant building into a music-focused arts centre that would bring new life into the old heart of the town. The brief included a 200-seat auditorium and dance studio, as well as a foyer, a bar and the usual backstage and administrative spaces. The challenge was to create these new facilities without making irreversible alterations to the historic fabric. Murphy's approach is the same as that of the Italian architect Carlo Scarpa (about whose work he has written fluently):

to juxtapose old and new boldly, even dramatically, with no elision of the two. The most important historic interior, the council room, was retained intact as a café and bar. Elsewhere in the building some quite radical alterations were eventually approved, for example the removal of one wall of the original courtroom to accommodate the new auditorium. The foyer sits below the auditorium gallery level, in the former courtyard.

Murphy's sense of drama is everywhere apparent: in the entry, through a gloomy vaulted tunnel; in the steel staircase and walkways, jagged and irregular in layout, that access the various levels of the building; and in the top-floor dance studio, occupying the attic of the old gaol, where new steel structures contrast with original timbers. There is a deliberate expressiveness about the project that some have found overemphasized. It is clear that the brief required a tight fit on a site with no potential for expansion, and the complex layout of the existing buildings, with many changes of level, provided an enormous challenge. The architects have responded with a scheme that is tough, brave and practical: a contrast to the timidity of much work of this kind in Britain.

Above
Richard Murphy's conversion of Stirling's historic Tolbooth grappled with the challenge of a complex plan to produce some impressive spaces, notably the top-floor dance studio.

Opposite
The scheme includes both radical new interventions, including a new steel stair, and careful restoration: the council room was retained intact as a café and bar.

WALES MILLENNIUM CENTRE, CARDIFF

PERCY THOMAS PARTNERSHIP, 1996–2004

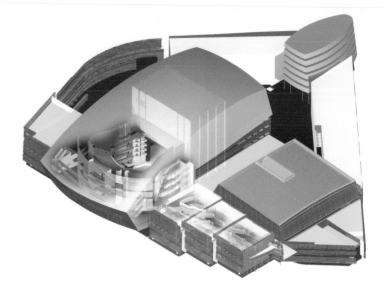

The Wales Millennium Centre, located on Cardiff's Pierhead and overlooking the Bristol Channel, stands on the site of one of the great 'unbuilts' of recent architectural history. The competition for a new opera house, a permanent base for the Welsh National Opera (WNO) and the focal point of the regeneration campaign for Cardiff's largely redundant docklands, was launched in 1993. The process was extended and marked by fierce controversy. Early in 1995 an outstanding scheme by Zaha Hadid, potentially a world-class building to rival the Guggenheim Museum in Bilbao, Spain, and even the Sydney Opera House in Australia, was selected. The abandonment of the Hadid scheme a year later, following its rejection by the Millennium Commission, was, according to former Secretary of State for Wales Nicholas Crickhowell, "a disaster for the arts in Britain and the people of Wales, and a personal tragedy for Zaha Hadid". Percy Thomas Partnership, a practice with its roots in Wales and which

had collaborated with Hadid on the competition submission, was subsequently appointed to design the Wales Millennium Centre on the same site.

The change of name was significant. Opera houses, it was claimed, in a country supposedly famed for its love of music, were élitist institutions. The brief for the Millennium Centre included accommodation for dance, literature and community theatre, and access for the disabled, as well as a 120-bed hostel for the Urdd (a Welsh youth organization) and offices and studios for the WNO. The centrepiece remains an 1800-seat lyric theatre that can be adapted to host performances from musicals or rock concerts to opera. After many tribulations, including the threat that the site would be sold to commercial developers, construction started early in 2002, with opening planned for 2004.

Percy Thomas Partnership's building is unlikely to be acclaimed as a major landmark of contemporary architecture

(although its distinctive form is in the spirit of Hadid, Will Alsop and Frank Gehry), but its completion will be significant for Wales. (The opera house fiasco was followed by the furore surrounding the proposed Welsh Assembly headquarters, designed by Richard Rogers.) The Wales Millennium Centre will be, the architects claim, "unmistakably Welsh". All materials have been sourced, as far as is possible, from within Wales, while the architects have paid scrupulous attention to the diversity and divisions, linguistic and economic, of a country in which the benefits of political devolution remain questionable. The building will be clad in slate from north Wales, with the main theatre encased in a patinated steel shell that emerges from the public concourse as a marker visible from afar. The lyric theatre is lined in handmade brick, with timber fronts to the balcony. The outcome of this earnest and deeply sincere project is keenly awaited.

Above
An 1800-seat lyric theatre is the centrepiece of the Wales Millennium Centre, which aims to reflect the breadth of Welsh cultural life.

Left
The building on the right is the Pierhead Building (offices of the Bute Docks) by William Frame, completed in 1896.

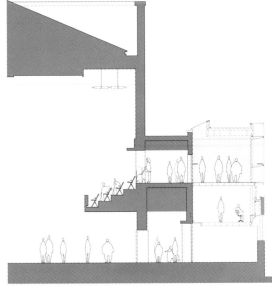

WOLVERHAMPTON CIVIC HALLS
WOLVERHAMPTON, WEST MIDLANDS
PENOYRE & PRASAD, 1996–2001

The practice of Lyons Israel Ellis Gray, as it was then known, was one of the most consistently interesting in 1950s and 1960s Britain. The firm had its origins, however, in Lyons & Israel's victory in the 1934 competition for a new civic hall at Wolverhampton. The young architects, subsequently adherents of the Modern Movement, turned to Classicism for that project, drawing inspiration from the stripped and streamlined Classical style of Scandinavian architecture and omitting the heavy detailing favoured by the stricter traditionalists of the period.

The building contains two concert halls, the Civic Hall and the smaller Wulfrun Hall, which have remained popular venues. The refurbishment project was generated by the need to re-equip the building to meet modern standards of safety, comfort and accessibility, while respecting its historic character, as it is now listed Grade II. Both the services and the internal décor were in need of renewal. Since the building is surrounded by streets on four sides, no extension was possible.

In addition to refurbishing the main hall, and increasing its capacity to 3000 by means of a new level of balconies, the project has provided greatly improved foyer and bar spaces – previously these were distinctly restricted – and new offices and dressing-rooms, as the originals were inadequate by modern standards. New floors have been added on all sides of the main auditorium. At mezzanine level there are offices, dressing-rooms and storage spaces. Above, contained within crystalline glass volumes, is a new level open to the public, with bars and WCs. The new additions have simple detailing, contrasting dramatically with the smooth masonry of the 1930s. By night, they glow, advertising the presence of the building. While the 1930s steel frame is concealed, Penoyre & Prasad's is partly exposed as a clear statement of its role. The careful restoration of the foyer, removing later accretions and repairing original features, incorporated the installation of a new disabled-access lift.

This project addresses the need to update a historic building in a bold and honest way, allowing the new additions to read clearly for what they are and making them worthy of their context. It is a model for the revitalization of many of Britain's basically sound, but tired, cultural facilities.

The comprehensive refurbishment of the Civic Halls included the addition of new audience facilities, contained within glazed volumes that form a marked contrast to the 1930s brickwork of Lyons & Israel's original building.

BENENDEN HOSPITAL, BENENDEN, KENT
JOHN McASLAN & PARTNERS

BIRMINGHAM CITY LIBRARY, BIRMINGHAM
RICHARD ROGERS PARTNERSHIP

CHELSEA COLLEGE OF ART AND DESIGN, LONDON SW1
ALLIES & MORRISON

DANCE BASE, EDINBURGH
MALCOLM FRASER ARCHITECTS

**HAMPDEN GURNEY PRIMARY SCHOOL
MARYLEBONE, LONDON NW1**
BUILDING DESIGN PARTNERSHIP

IDEA STORE, WHITECHAPEL, LONDON E1
ADJAYE ASSOCIATES

JUBILEE PRIMARY SCHOOL, TULSE HILL, LONDON SW2
ALLFORD HALL MONAGHAN MORRIS

LABAN CENTRE, DEPTFORD, LONDON SE8
HERZOG & DE MEURON

MAGGIE'S CENTRES, VARIOUS LOCATIONS
VARIOUS PRACTICES

**MEDICAL AND DENTAL SCHOOL, QUEEN MARY COLLEGE
UNIVERSITY OF LONDON, WHITECHAPEL, LONDON E1**
ALSOP ARCHITECTS

NORTH END NURSERY, BEXLEY, KENT
BIRDS PORTCHMOUTH RUSSUM

**PANOPTICAN BUILDING, UNIVERSITY COLLEGE LONDON
LONDON WC1**
JEREMY DIXON.EDWARD JONES

**ROTHERMERE AMERICAN INSTITUTE
UNIVERSITY OF OXFORD, OXFORDSHIRE**
KOHN PEDERSEN FOX

**SAID BUSINESS SCHOOL, UNIVERSITY OF OXFORD
OXFORDSHIRE**
JEREMY DIXON.EDWARD JONES

STUDENT CENTRE, QUEEN'S UNIVERSITY, BELFAST
JEREMY DIXON.EDWARD JONES/BUILDING DESIGN PARTNERSHIP

**TANAKA BUSINESS SCHOOL, IMPERIAL COLLEGE
SOUTH KENSINGTON, LONDON SW7**
FOSTER AND PARTNERS

**TELEVISION, THEATRE AND FILM STUDIES BUILDING
UNIVERSITY OF WALES, ABERYSTWYTH**
PATEL TAYLOR

TRINITY COLLEGE OF MUSIC, GREENWICH, LONDON SE10
JOHN McASLAN & PARTNERS

BENENDEN HOSPITAL, BENENDEN, KENT

JOHN McASLAN & PARTNERS, 1999–2003

John McAslan & Partners has refurbished and upgraded a number of classic modern buildings, for example the De La Warr Pavilion at Bexhill-on-Sea, East Sussex, the Peter Jones department store in Sloane Square, London, and even a campus in Florida, USA, designed by Frank Lloyd Wright. At Benenden Hospital, Kent, the practice was called on to replace a poor-quality 1950s ward block with a new clinical facility, and to restore the integrity of an adjacent 1930s listed building damaged by the 1950s project.

The listed sanatorium block, designed for the care of tuberculosis patients, was completed in 1937 to designs by Burnet, Tait & Lorne. It is a dynamic and elegant Modernist structure, probably influenced by Erich Mendelsohn and Serge Chermayeff's De La Warr Pavilion. The construction of the 1953 ward building, in a diluted version of Burnet, Tait & Lorne's style, involved the partial demolition of the 1937 building, with one of the distinctive curved ends removed to make way for a clumsy link block.

The project has restored the original form of the listed building, and added a link building connecting new and old. The new clinic, on a slightly realigned site, provides a radical contrast to its neighbour: no attempt is made to mimic the Modern manner of the 1930s. It is a rigorously detailed pavilion in steel and glass, with ample sun-shading to ensure internal comfort.

Above
The new clinic at Benenden Hospital stands adjacent to a listed 1930s block by Burnet, Tait & Lorne.

Opposite
The new building, a simple, glazed pavilion, with ample solar-screening on its southern elevation, is in the spirit of the 1930s block, which has itself been repaired and refurbished.

BIRMINGHAM CITY LIBRARY, BIRMINGHAM

RICHARD ROGERS PARTNERSHIP, 2002–

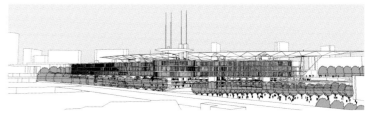

The proposed new library by Richard Rogers Partnership (RRP) is a major ingredient in the regeneration strategy for Birmingham's Eastside. Although close to the city centre, the area has suffered from the isolation imposed by the reconstruction of Birmingham during the 1960s, with an urban motorway forming a tight collar around the central core. The masterplan for Eastside, developed by HOK, seeks to reintegrate the area into the city; Nicholas Grimshaw's Millennium Point is a recent addition, reflecting the new identity of the area as an education and knowledge quarter.

A competition for the new library in Eastside was won by RRP in 2002. The existing central library, close to the council house, is itself a product of the 1960s, a powerful but rather intimidating design by John Madin that replaced a splendid (and much lamented) Victorian building by J.H. Chamberlain. The Madin library is to be demolished and the site sold for commercial development.

The brief for the new building incorporated a vision of the public library of the future as a learning resource for all, open and inviting, and utilizing a wide range of media. It must also provide for one of Britain's largest reference collections, which includes many rare books, manuscripts and photographs.

The RRP scheme captures the idea of the new library as a cultural landmark and symbol of renewal. The vesica-shaped building stands in a new green park, part of a progression of public parks forming

a pedestrian route through the area. The library is contained under a great roof, a spreading canopy incorporating a 'sky roof' and supported on structural trees, which extends over the surrounding landscape. The library floors are flexible spaces sheltering below the roof. The reference collection is housed on the top three floors, with lending library, exhibition spaces, foyers, auditorium and children's library (opening on to a large terrace/play deck) located below. The diagram places storage and stack areas at the heart of the building, with working areas around the edge, where visitors can enjoy views out to the park.

A separate block of accommodation, or co-locator building, will provide an acoustic barrier against the elevated railway viaduct nearby. It could in principle contain a wide range of cultural and community activities – artists' studios, a school of speech and drama, a primary healthcare trust, a national academy of writing and other compatible academic/training/learning activities. A covered galleria extends between this building and the library and forms part of the pedestrian route through Eastside.

The Birmingham City Library, likely to be the first significant Rogers building completed in a British provincial city, is a dazzling product of a practice that remains one of the powerhouses of architecture in Britain. The project equally reflects Richard Rogers's own passionate campaign for the revival of city life and will reinforce Birmingham's claims as one of the leaders of this process.

Set in a new city park, Richard Rogers's City Library is a key component in the campaign to regenerate Birmingham's Eastside. A covered gallery extends through the building.

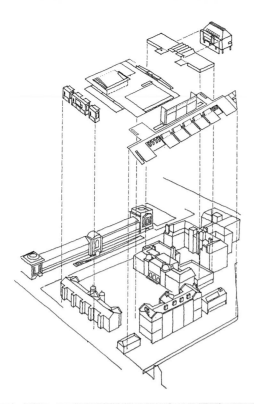

CHELSEA COLLEGE OF ART AND DESIGN
LONDON SW1

ALLIES & MORRISON, 2001–05

The decision to remove the Royal Army Medical College from its site on Millbank, London, next to Tate Britain, inaugurated a period of bidding for the site from a number of potential users. Fortunately, the London Institute, which incorporates Chelsea College, was the successful bidder. The college is to be relocated there, and its former premises in Chelsea sold for development. The London Institute will also move its central administration to Millbank.

Allies & Morrison (which had recently completed a major landscaping scheme at Tate Britain and had also worked for the London College of Printing, part of the London Institute) was appointed in 2001 to prepare a masterplan for the site. Three listed buildings – handsome late Victorian structures of brick with stone dressings – are to be extended to the rear to house

studios, offices, a library and a restaurant. Alterations to the interiors will be minimal, as the spaces are highly suitable for the new use. The focus of the new campus will be the former parade ground (used in recent years as a car park). This is to become a public square, open to all, with a new gallery underneath. It would be practically possible, at some future date, to connect this with the basement level of the nearby Tate.

This project is central to the idea of a new arts quarter around the Tate, which for too long has been an isolated cultural presence in this part of London; Tate Britain is itself looking at further expansion plans. It provides an ideal commission for Allies & Morrison, whose fastidious, understated approach is unlikely to jar in the context of the listed buildings and conservation area.

Allies & Morrison's additions to the former Royal Army Medical College consist of extensions to the existing listed buildings. Gallery spaces will be formed under the former parade ground, which is to be developed as a public square.

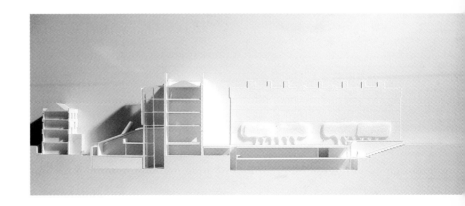

DANCE BASE, EDINBURGH

MALCOLM FRASER ARCHITECTS, 1998–2002

Dance Base is a remarkable response to the dramatic geography and dense historic townscape of the Scottish capital. The site is off the Grassmarket, on the lower slopes of the Castle Rock. The new building wraps around existing buildings, opening up neglected backlands left vacant after the old residential closes were demolished as part of nineteenth- and early twentieth-century slum clearance programmes. This strikingly contemporary project offers a new view of one of Europe's finest historic cities.

Four studios were created in which up to 200,000 people annually of all ages and abilities, from beginners to accomplished professionals, can enjoy dance as an educational, social and recreational art form. There are workshops for professional dancers, and programmes for young children and the disabled. The principal studio space has a large glazed roof that offers stunning views up to the castle. A second, located in a converted building, faces south on to the Grassmarket with its shops and bars, and a third has big timber doors opening on to a tranquil green space. The fourth studio is excavated out of the Castle Rock itself. Each studio has a distinct character. Terraces, decks and gardens reach out of the building to the sky and the views, while lifts, stairs and ramps connect the levels within it. Despite the complexity of the site, the building is remarkably legible.

Above
Dance Base occupies a steeply sloping site off Edinburgh's Grassmarket.

Right
Internal spaces have a toughness and rigour in the local tradition.

Opposite
Studio spaces are top-lit, with striking views of the castle from the upper levels of the building.

HAMPDEN GURNEY PRIMARY SCHOOL, MARYLEBONE, LONDON W1

BUILDING DESIGN PARTNERSHIP, 1995–2002

Sir Arthur Conan Doyle's fictional detective Sherlock Holmes famously referred to the board schools of Victorian London as "beacons of the future". Towering above the humble terraced streets and often with playgrounds on the roof, these citadels of learning, according to Holmes, presaged a more civilized society.

Building Design Partnership's (BDP) Hampden Gurney Primary School, located in Marylebone, London, marks, in one sense, a return to tradition. Post-war schools, even in inner London, have tended to be low-rise, but Hampden Gurney, like the old board schools, is a multi-level school and has playing areas set high above the streets. Yet in other respects – in its transparency, lightness and flexibility – it is a radical design, far removed from the rigidly compartmented academies of the nineteenth century.

The site was formerly occupied by a typical low-rise school of the 1950s, built inexpensively on land cleared by wartime bombing – a gash in the densely built-up area. Plans for a new school came to fruition in 1995, when BDP was appointed to design it after competitive interviews. The school itself is now framed by two housing blocks, also designed by BDP, that help to cement it into its context and were vital to the funding package.

The diagram of the building is clear and practical. The ground floor contains a nursery area, plus offices and staff room. From here, pupils progress literally 'up the school': the top floor has a technology garden for those in year six. An assembly hall and a chapel (since this is a Church of England school) are located at basement level, together with a playground for ball games. Other play areas, which can be used for open-air teaching in fine weather, are provided on the street front at each level. They are connected to the classrooms by bridges across the void that extends through the centre of the building and is a source of natural ventilation. A tensile fabric canopy extends above the atrium and provides some shelter for the rooftop play area. The openness of the steel-framed building reflects some skilful structural engineering (also by BDP), with a roof-top bow arch picking up the floor loadings.

Directly commissioned by the end-user, this school shows that private finance initiatives (PFIs) are not the only, or the best, way to procure new education buildings. In Paris there would be nothing remarkable about Hampden Gurney; in London, it is a revelation – the best new school in the capital for some years. This makes the delays imposed by the local authority, Westminster City Council – planning permission took three years to secure – all the more lamentable.

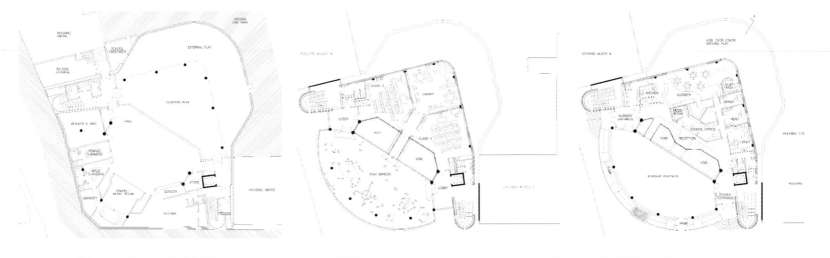

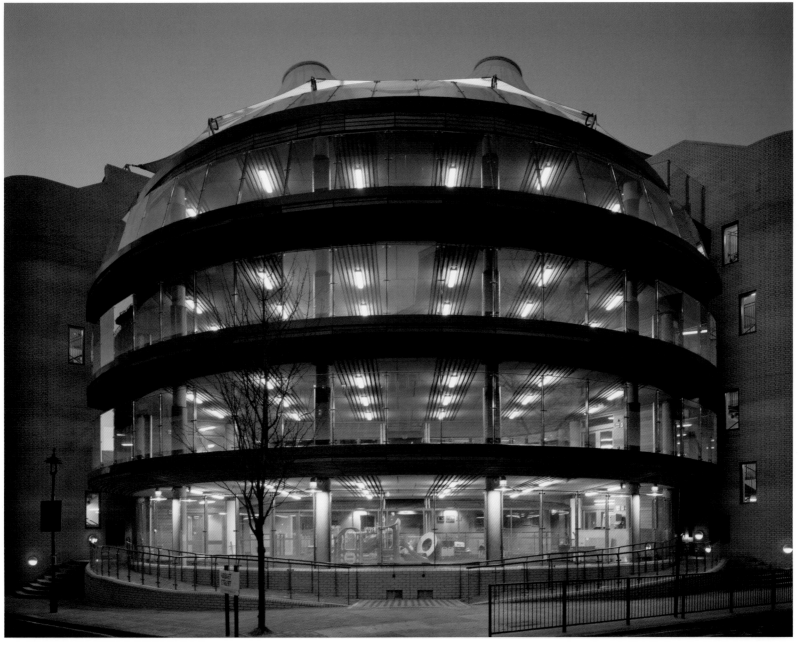

IDEA STORE, WHITECHAPEL, LONDON E1

ADJAYE ASSOCIATES, 2001–04

Above
The building is clad in a mix of clear and coloured glazing and glass-faced aluminium panels.

Opposite
The project aims to 'demystify' the public library and attract new users to a building that offers entertainment alongside enlightenment.

The Idea Store project – actually a public library, designed for Tower Hamlets Council – is a significant landmark for David Adjaye. His rapid rise to prominence has been achieved on the basis of exhibition fit-outs (for example, at the Design Museum and Victoria Miro Gallery, both in London) and lavish domestic interiors, followed by the sensational Elektra House and, more recently, the Dirty House (see pp. 158–59), also both in London. The important public commission for the Idea Store will be a test of Adjaye's ability to work on a large scale and to a tight budget. (Early in 2003 Adjaye was shortlisted for the design of the new British Embassy in Warsaw, Poland – an achievement in itself for a young architect.)

The Idea Store concept clearly develops the philosophy of Will Alsop's Peckham Library in south London, in terms of updating the idea of the public library to fit in with contemporary attitudes and lifestyles. The aim is to demystify it: the way to get people into libraries, it is argued, is to build them in shopping hubs and run them like shops. A library should be not just a repository of knowledge and information, but an active presence in the community,

linked to lifelong learning programmes, that attracts people who would not usually visit such an institution.

The Whitechapel Idea Store forms part of the frontage of one of the East End's main thoroughfares. The five-storey building has shops at street level, with the remainder of the 4500-square-metre (48,440-square-foot) floor space consisting of flexible areas in which library and education spaces are mixed. The façade does more than enclose the floors: the curtain wall of coloured and clear glazing and glass-faced aluminium panels is envisaged as a medium for displaying information. (The idea is hardly new: Rogers & Piano wanted to make the piazza frontage of the Pompidou Centre, Paris, into an electronic noticeboard; they were inspired in turn by Oscar Nitschke's unbuilt Maison de la Publicité project of the 1930s.) Inside there is a full-height atrium extending out over the pavement and containing stairs and escalators to draw people up the building. The top floor contains a café with spectacular views over the City and East End. If all this does not demystify the library, nothing ever will.

JUBILEE PRIMARY SCHOOL, TULSE HILL
LONDON SW2

ALLFORD HALL MONAGHAN MORRIS, 2000–02

A project won in competition by Allford Hall Monaghan Morris (AHMM), the Jubilee Primary School follows on from the practice's much-discussed school at Great Notley in Essex, completed in 1999 and particularly notable for its sustainable servicing strategy.

The Jubilee Primary School was commissioned by Lambeth Council as one of four large new primary schools in the south London borough. The site was formerly occupied by Brockwell Primary School but was far from large. Apart from the main 420-pupil infant and primary school, it had to accommodate a special-needs unit for deaf children and a crèche for children under three years old. Facilities for the local community also had to be provided.

The success of the project is rooted in its strong diagram, with the hall (widely used by local people outside school hours) forming a dramatic presence on the street; a blue brick wall marks the main entrance to the school. The classrooms are arranged in a single block along the northern edge of the site: juniors are on the first floor, nursery and infant classes below. Playground areas can be accessed directly from both levels. The special-needs unit is located at the quietest corner of the site, with its own entrance. The southern part of the site is devoted to open play areas.

Low running costs were a prime objective: light and ventilation chimneys serve the classrooms. Recycled materials have been widely used, and the classroom block has an insulating sedum roof.

The school's showpiece status was reinforced by the commissioning of Studio Myerscough to develop signage and a brand identity, and of Andrew Stafford to design bespoke furniture. Artist Martin Richman collaborated with the architects on a number of elements in the scheme. The school was an appropriate project for completion during the royal Golden Jubilee year of 2002. Fifty years ago schools – for example, Bousfield School, South Kensington, by Chamberlin, Powell & Bon, and Hallfield School, Bayswater, by Denys Lasdun – were among the finest products of the post-war renewal programme. AHMM's building is worthy to stand comparison with these iconic works.

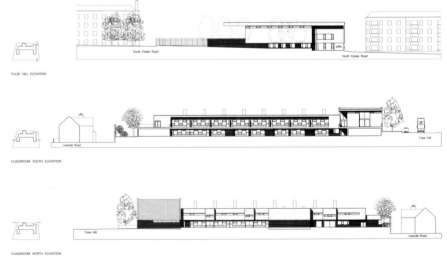

LABAN CENTRE, DEPTFORD, LONDON SE8

HERZOG & DE MEURON, 1997–2003

Below
The Laban Centre can be read as a creative 'village', with internal 'streets' facilitating social interaction as well as circulation.

Opposite
Externally an ethereal presence, the Laban is internally generous in scale and built for hard wear. A colour scheme by Michael Craig-Martin reinforces the sense of place.

Herzog & de Meuron's Laban Centre is a unique building housing a unique institution. Named after Rudolf Laban (1879–1958), 'the father of modern dance', the centre operated for nearly thirty years from a sprawl of converted buildings in New Cross, a few miles from its new Thameside site at Deptford Creek (formerly a refuse tip). Its removal to Deptford is a component in the strategy to regenerate the area, which was once a centre of shipbuilding – and boasts one of London's finest Baroque churches, Thomas Archer's St Paul's – but is now one of London's poorest districts.

Herzog & de Meuron's 1997 competition victory (Peter Zumthor, Enric Miralles, David Chipperfield and Tony Fretton were among other contenders) came at a time when their Tate Modern project in London was moving from design to construction. Following delays in securing Heritage Lottery funding, the centre was constructed in 2000–02 and formally opened early in 2003.

On a superficial level, the centre can be read as a shed in the local tradition, raised above the mundane by its bold use of external colour (in the form of polycarbonate sheets fixed in front of the glazed façade panels). The revelatory qualities of the building, however, are to be found beyond the façades. The interior is planned around three 'wedges' of circulation space, internal streets intended to encourage creative interaction and a memory of the rambling (but well-loved) collection of buildings that the centre formerly inhabited. Internal courts bring natural light deep into the building and allow views across it. Studios (a total of thirteen, none strictly rectangular) are arranged around the perimeter, while a 300-seat theatre, a facility the centre hitherto lacked, fills the centre of the building. The cafeteria and library are placed along its creekside edge. Two hefty spiral staircases, painted black, provide the principal means of vertical circulation and are seen as places for social encounters. The centre is big-boned, generous and tough, designed to take hard wear from a teaching and learning community that is used to hard work and long hours. This is a creative 'village', intended to reinforce the Laban's established sense of community. The client, led by the centre's director, Marion North, had a strong input in the development of the scheme.

Colour was a vital ingredient from the beginning. Artist Michael Craig-Martin (whom the architects first encountered as a trustee of the Tate) was brought in at an early stage and the strong hues he chose give a sense of orientation and identity to the internal spaces.

Herzog & de Meuron has never been the 'minimalist' practice that some imagine, but the Laban reflects an increasingly expressive element in its architecture that recalls, in some respects, the work of the German architect Hans Scharoun. The full impact of the centre will be evident when the remarkable landscape scheme (by Gunther Vogt) is complete, but it can already be regarded as one of the few really significant buildings generated by the cultural building boom of the 1990s.

MAGGIE'S CENTRES, VARIOUS LOCATIONS
VARIOUS PRACTICES, 1996–

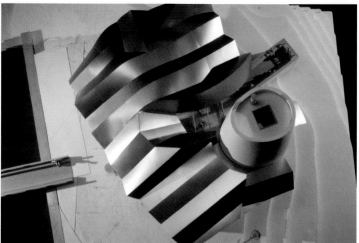

Maggie Keswick Jencks, wife of the architectural critic Charles Jencks, died of cancer in 1995. Her experience of battling with the disease convinced her that cancer patients need not only conventional medical treatment, but also information, advice and solace. Ideally these should be provided in buildings close to, but distinctly independent of, the hospitals where patients are being treated. If all goes to plan, there will be thirteen such centres in Britain by 2008, including buildings by Frank Gehry, Zaha Hadid and Daniel Libeskind – a truly remarkable programme in architectural, as well as healthcare, terms.

Edinburgh's Western General Hospital, where Maggie Jencks had been treated, was a natural choice for the first Maggie's Centre, opened in 1996, which is now used by over 16,000 people annually. In his radical conversion of a disused stable block in the grounds of the Edinburgh hospital, donated by the hospital authority, Richard Murphy created a wonderfully colourful, comfortable and welcoming space. In 2000–01 he extended the centre, at a cost of under £250,000, virtually doubling it in size and providing office, consulting-room and meeting-room spaces. A Millennium Lottery grant provided a fillip for the idea of building more centres.

As befits an organization of which Charles Jencks, the prophet of architectural

pluralism, is a trustee, the charitable trust that runs the development programme for future centres has gone to a wide variety of architectural practices for designs. In Glasgow, Page & Park was the choice; in Dundee it was Frank Gehry. Richard Rogers is working on a scheme for London's Charing Cross Hospital. Zaha Hadid's building will be in Kirkcaldy. Further centres are planned for Sheffield, Nottingham, Oxford, Swansea, Cambridge and Cheltenham, in addition to two further Scottish locations. More could follow: cancer is now the major killer disease, and a local newspaper appeal quickly raised £500,000 to fund the Glasgow centre. Maggie's Centres are, typically, converted buildings, costing around £750,000 to construct – very small beer for an architect of Gehry's fame.

The project is driven by Charles Jencks's conviction – shared by his late wife – that the environment in which sick people are treated matters a great deal. Architecture cannot cure cancer, but a stimulating and welcoming place can help people fight the disease and live longer. Health buildings are too often purely functional, but survival and recovery are not entirely predictable processes. Maggie's Centres are a potent statement about the place of fine architecture in the campaign to tackle disease.

The Maggie's Centre in Dundee (*right*) is Gehry's first building in Britain. Opened in 2003, it features a concertina roof of steel and timber. Maggie's Centre Fife in Kirkcaldy (*opposite*) has been designed by Zaha Hadid and is scheduled to open in 2004.

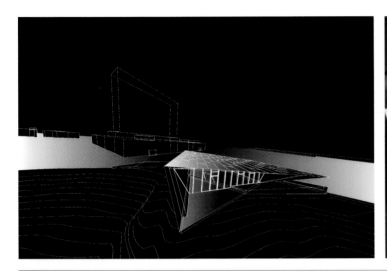

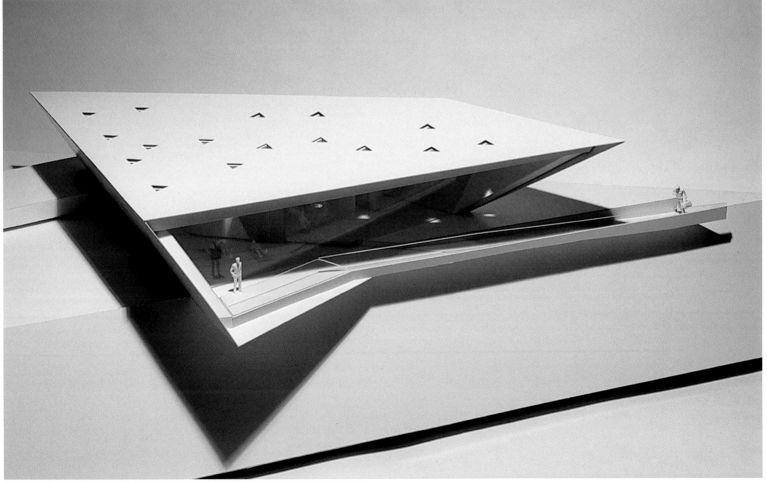

MEDICAL AND DENTAL SCHOOL
QUEEN MARY COLLEGE, UNIVERSITY OF LONDON
WHITECHAPEL, LONDON E1

ALSOP ARCHITECTS, 2001–04

Will Alsop's new medical school includes an interactive science centre (*above*), open to the public and visible within the glazed pavilion of the building. The building is innovative in its provision of interactive space (*opposite*) – vital in a modern research facility – and breaks with the idea of medical buildings as anonymous and secretive.

Will Alsop's new medical and dental school for Queen Mary College, University of London, will house the combined schools of St Bartholomew's and the Royal London hospitals on a site adjacent to the latter in Whitechapel, east London. The building, with 9000 square metres (96,880 square feet) of floor space, will contain research laboratories, teaching spaces, lecture theatres, offices and a café, as well as an innovative interactive science centre intended to be used by local schools. This will be the first publicly accessible facility within any British medical school – perhaps a place where the doctors of the future will discover their vocation.

Medical schools, like hospitals, are specialized buildings, usually designed by practices with extensive experience in the field. As a result they are often dire architecturally. For this project Alsop teamed up with AMEC and drew on the latter's expertise in laboratory design to produce a scheme that transforms the image of medical buildings as drab and anonymous. This school is intended as a statement of the dynamic nature of medical research, a place where traditional barriers are removed.

The heart of the building is, in fact, a public space or 'street' overlooked by the café – further reflecting the move to involve the local community in medical research and teaching – and flanked by a great wall of services. All laboratory space is concentrated on one huge floorplate at lower-ground level, extending across the entire site. Specialist research laboratories occupy enclosed cells around the open-plan teaching areas. The glazed pavilion, clad with a double-skin curtain wall, that gives the building its potent presence on the street contains write-up, seminar and office areas on three upper floors. Alsop's characteristic pods and free-form spaces allow views through the building and encourage interaction and socialization by students and staff. The science centre stands within the pavilion, clearly visible from the outside. A 400-seat lecture theatre is sited on the opposite side of the central street. The building is intended as "a backdrop of light and art" to the very serious activities that it houses, but it is a highly practical container, designed for flexibility in the rapidly changing world of research. It should be a place of inspiration: it could be one of the most exciting London buildings of the early twenty-first century, and it is particularly encouraging that it is sited in London's East End.

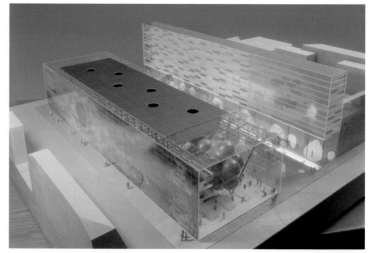

NORTH END NURSERY, BEXLEY, KENT

BIRDS PORTCHMOUTH RUSSUM, 2002–

This project reflects the proactive role being taken by the Commission for Architecture and the Built Environment (CABE) in promoting innovative design. CABE organized a competition on behalf of the Department for Education and Skills (DES) for a new nursery to be built on a brownfield site at Bexley, Kent. It is very much a demonstration project, exemplifying the ideas that the DES is seeking to instil into new nursery schools.

The winning submission, by Birds Portchmouth Russum (BPR), proposed a building that is durable, economical, welcoming and child-centred. Its site is used partly for car parking, though it is close to parkland. The nursery, clad in coloured steel panels, is set within a circular enclosure, a 'toy fort' constructed of recycled railway sleepers inclined outwards to deter climbers. Inside the enclosure is a tree-lined forecourt, which acts as a place for parents to gather as children arrive at or leave the nursery. The central space in the building is a top-lit play

and dining area. From here three wings of cellular accommodation extend, overlooking three enclosed open-air courtyards, each specifically designed for the needs of babies, toddlers and other pre-school children, and equipped with retractable awnings to provide protection from rain and sun. The glazed entrance lobby gives access to two community rooms, used by local residents outside school hours.

This is a building designed to be comfortable and hard-wearing. Coloured rubber flooring is used throughout the interior, with cork in the play areas. The use of controlled natural light and natural ventilation reduces its running costs.

BPR is a practice that genuinely regards every project as a fresh challenge and an opportunity to rethink the role of architecture. It has realized too few buildings, but it is to be hoped that this will be the first of many of its completed works in the new century.

The North End Nursery is conceived as a 'toy fort' within which play areas and community spaces are arranged around open courtyards.

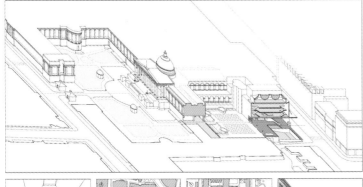

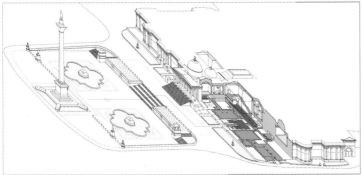

PANOPTICON BUILDING
UNIVERSITY COLLEGE LONDON, LONDON WC1
JEREMY DIXON.EDWARD JONES, 2002–

University College London (UCL) was founded in 1826, and its original buildings (by William Wilkins) form a handsome Classical quadrangle off Gower Street. The college subsequently expanded to fill the entire area between Gower Street and Gordon Square, and has also colonized the surrounding streets. The site for the Panopticon Building is the last significant space left for new building on UCL's core site. Left empty for over half a century after wartime bombing, it is a glaring gap between the handsome Victorian terrace on the west side of Gordon Square and the 1960s Bloomsbury Theatre on Gordon Street, a bold composition that paid little regard to its context.

The new building has two clear functions: first, to house a number of badly needed new facilities for the college, and, secondly, to form a dignified gateway to UCL from the west, as part of a comprehensible route across the site. It will house collections of rare books and manuscripts, and the Petrie Collection of Egyptian antiquities, on four upper floors (with two levels of basement storage), and provide a lecture theatre, cinema, gallery and restaurant, open to all, at ground- and first-floor levels.

The composition of the façade consists of a blank, windowless, three-storey zone, representing the hidden nature of the Petrie Collection, above a glazed ground floor that represents the new entrance to the university campus from the east. A substantial canopy marking the entrance extends over the pavement, providing a place for students to gather. The stone will be a form of dark granite that was used by the ancient Egyptians and comes from the area of the Valley of the Kings in Egypt. The dark colour of the façade will pick up the general tone of the façade to Gordon Square, and will allow the interior to be read as a dramatic contrast and as an invitation to use the new route through UCL. The top of the building, above the dark stone, will be polychromatic and set back, with a build-up of volume towards the higher profile of the Bloomsbury Theatre.

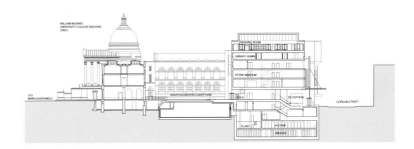

The Panopticon forms an extension to UCL's original complex of buildings by William Wilkins. The building fills a gap created by wartime bombing, with the bold mass of the 1960s Bloomsbury Theatre as a neighbour.

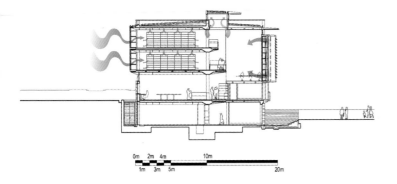

ROTHERMERE AMERICAN STUDIES INSTITUTE
UNIVERSITY OF OXFORD, OXFORDSHIRE

KOHN PEDERSEN FOX, 1994–2001

0m 2m 4m   10m
1m 3m 5m   20m

Kohn Pedersen Fox (KPF), founded in New York in 1976, began working in Britain in the boom years of the late 1980s and in 1990 established an office in London that has subsequently developed as a virtually autonomous practice, with projects in many European countries. KPF is best known for its office buildings, which made its victory in the 1994 competition for the University of Oxford's American Studies Institute all the more significant. In 2002 it was appointed to design a new residential block for St Anne's College, Oxford.

The site for the institute – construction of which began only in 1999 – was within the gardens of Mansfield College and close to Rhodes House (with its established American connections), outside the historic centre of Oxford but in a highly sensitive locale. Architecture in Oxford in recent decades has moved away from the uncompromising toughness of James Stirling's Florey Building, Arne Jacobsen's St Catherine's College and Ahrends, Burton & Koralek's additions to Keble College. It now favours a history-conscious contextualism exemplified by Richard MacCormac's additions to St John's College and reaching its zenith in Demetri Porphyrios's eccentric extension to Magdalen College. KPF's American Studies Institute vigorously eschews the latter tendency: its contextualism is of a subtler variety.

The diagram of the building takes its cue from the adjacent library of Mansfield College designed by Basil Champneys, with a lofty reading-room set above an undercroft containing subsidiary spaces. The steel-framed reading-room is a lightweight structure, contrasting with the solid concrete, stone-clad construction of the undercroft. It has a glazed elevation overlooking the garden of Mansfield College, and since it faces south this façade is fully equipped with sunshade louvres. Inside, two levels of study carrels overlook the central space, like boxes in a theatre. Book stacks are located to the rear: the solid north façade faces on to the backs of adjacent buildings. The undercroft contains studies and seminar rooms, some of which open directly on to the garden. An elegant glazed tower at the east end of the building provides a compositional balance to the stone-faced 'bookend' at the west.

KPF was told by the client that it had secured the job *despite*, rather than because of, its American origins. It is not only the appropriateness of the elegant pavilion (with its roots in Pierre Chareau's Maison de Verre in Paris) for the site that impresses. The building is finely crafted and fastidiously detailed – all in all, a remarkable Oxford début by this practice.

Opposite
KPF's Rothermere American Studies Institute occupies a site in the gardens of Mansfield College; its diagram is that of Champneys' college library.

Above
The reading-room is set above an undercroft containing studies and seminar rooms, with book stacks to the rear.

Right
Controlled natural light makes the reading-room a luminous space.

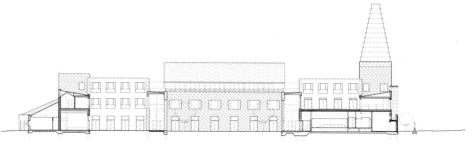

SAID BUSINESS SCHOOL
UNIVERSITY OF OXFORD, OXFORDSHIRE

JEREMY DIXON.EDWARD JONES, 1996–2001

Dixon.Jones won the limited competition for the University of Oxford's new business school in July 1996. The site was at that time a playing field on Mansfield Road in the leafy Parks area of the city. The proposal to build there proved highly controversial and was referred to the university's Congregation, which voted down the scheme. Only in 1999 did construction start, on a new site, next to Oxford railway station, with the project radically rethought. The building was opened in autumn 2001.

The new site was potentially daunting: it was located on the messy fringe of the city centre, next to the dismal modern station and its untidy forecourt and facing a busy highway. In response, Dixon.Jones abandoned the romantic informality of the scheme intended for the Parks area, and produced a strongly urban alternative that has clear roots in the Italian Rationalism and stripped Classicism of the inter-war years. Not for Oxford, however, was there to be a business school resembling a routine office block. With the encouragement of principal donor Wafic Said, the architects produced a building with real, perhaps even overstated, monumentality that easily dominates its mundane surroundings. The main material is brick, relieved by a certain amount of natural stone, creating a solid wall of masonry against the external world; the roofs are made of zinc or copper. What other architect (or client) would have dared propose an addition to Oxford's skyline of 'dreaming spires'? Yet Dixon.Jones has built such a spire: a copper-clad ziggurat, inspired by the work of Nicholas Hawksmoor, that conceals the vents for the heat-exchange system and is just as memorable as Oxford's other recent spire, that of Nuffield College.

The layout of the school is essentially collegiate, in contrast to other recent faculty buildings at Oxford, although there is, of course, no residential accommodation. The aim was, perhaps, to give the students – typically mature in years and often part-time in attendance – a base with a real sense of identity and community. The heart of the place is a green quadrangle, 60 x 30 metres (200 x 100 feet), surrounded by spacious glazed cloisters. Smaller, enclosed courts on the east side of the building contain two storeys of seminar rooms. Along the west side four large Harvard University-style lecture theatres are topped by more open courts, overlooked by studies for academics. In contrast to the typically accretive form of the Oxford college, the plan is as rational as the architecture, a model of symmetry and order. The relatively large budget allowed for exceptionally generous amounts of circulation and social space: informal interaction is seen as fundamental to the students' experience of the school.

The building is entered via a sheltered, partly enclosed *porte-cochère* from the busy street. With its costly stone flooring and chairs designed by Ludwig Mies van der Rohe the entrance area has an unmistakably corporate feel, but why should a business school not feel corporate? Where an international bank would place the dealing floor, however, there is the great quadrangle, culminating to the north in an open-air amphitheatre – a formal gesture, perhaps, rather than a practical amenity. Below are the common-room and restaurant.

For some – including those in the university who believe that business studies do not belong in Oxford – the Said Business School is an alien intruder into a cherished scene. Its opulence confirms the impression that it is a rich man's fancy. Yet the building has made a more positive contribution to the city centre than any new development of the last half century and is a major work by a practice that pursues, with extraordinary virtuosity, a decidedly alternative version of the modern tradition. It is as an interface between tradition and modernity, in terms both of its architecture and of the new approaches to teaching and learning that it houses, that the Said School has made its mark on Oxford.

Above
The highly rational diagram of the Said Business School focuses on a central quadrangle surrounded by cloisters – like an Italian *campo santo*.

Opposite
Located in a mundane area of Oxford, the building is essentially inward-looking, with generous and calm spaces that merge traditional and modern themes.

STUDENT CENTRE
QUEEN'S UNIVERSITY, BELFAST

JEREMY DIXON.EDWARD JONES/
BUILDING DESIGN PARTNERSHIP, 2001–

Queen's University in Belfast is located in an attractive Victorian suburban quarter – now largely a conservation area – close to the city centre.

Its new student centre was the subject of a limited competition in 2001, won by Dixon.Jones working with the Belfast office of Building Design Partnership (BDP). The site is directly opposite Sir Charles Lanyon's original Queen's College, an elaborate neo-Tudor composition, on University Road.

The brief was for a complex that will be far more than a student union: open to staff, students and the local community, it contains shops, bars, a restaurant, common rooms, a nightclub and music venue, and accommodation for societies and clubs. In urban terms the building marks a point of transition between the open lawns of the Lanyon campus and the regular grid of streets, already colonized by the university, behind University Road to the west. The architects responded to its location by

creating a building that is both a destination and a route. Its heart is a linear square, covered by a glazed roof carried on tall steel columns and enclosed by two four-storey blocks of accommodation, connected by bridges, along the north and south sides. The square is entered through a façade of sheer glazing, protected from solar gain by the oversailing roof. The building is externally stone-clad and deliberately formal, even monumental, in its aspect to University Road, but tailored to

the more modest street scene where it faces on to the adjacent Elmwood Avenue.

While entirely lacking explicit historical references, the building has Classical roots: its formality is a response to its setting. The project is linked to plans for significantly recasting the landscape around the Lanyon building and University Road, and reinforcing the area's identity as an informal urban campus.

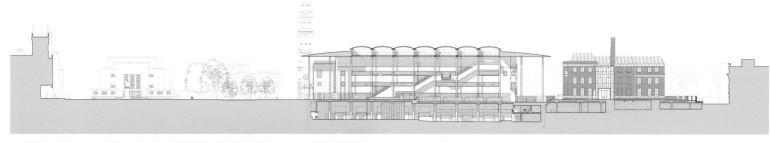

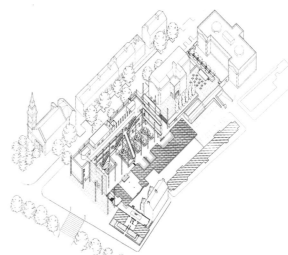

TANAKA BUSINESS SCHOOL, IMPERIAL COLLEGE
SOUTH KENSINGTON, LONDON SW7

FOSTER AND PARTNERS, 2002–04

Imperial College – effectively the British equivalent of the Massachusetts Institute of Technology – occupies a crowded site in South Kensington, London, between the Albert Hall and the Science and Natural History museums. During the 1960s T.E. Collcutt's magnificent Imperial Institute, except for its landmark tower, was demolished to allow for the expansion of the college. Some fine town houses by the late nineteenth-century architect Richard Norman Shaw were also flattened. Unfortunately, most of the new buildings subsequently developed by Imperial College were of mediocre quality. In more recent years the college has raised its sights: John McAslan has refurbished and extended the library, for example.

Foster and Partners' involvement with the college developed from the practice's work early in the 1990s on Albertopolis, a masterplan for the entire South Kensington museum and education quarter. As part of a subsequent development plan for Imperial College, Foster designed the Sir Alexander Fleming Building (1994–98), a structure of outstanding quality housing medical research and teaching facilities. The next Foster addition was the Flowers Building, containing multi-disciplinary research space and slotted into a tight backland site adjacent to the Science Museum's Wellcome Wing.

The Tanaka Business School, in contrast, is prominently located on Exhibition Road: the project is linked to a radical reconstruction of the college's main entrance. Part of the accommodation is contained within a refurbished 1920s block, while a new stainless-steel drum, housing banks of lecture rooms and set in a landscaped court, will be an arresting addition to the streetscape.

Above left
Foster and Partners' work at Imperial College includes the Sir Alexander Fleming Building, completed in 1998.

Left
The Tanaka Business School gives the college a striking new 'front door' on Exhibition Road.

TELEVISION, THEATRE AND FILM STUDIES BUILDING
UNIVERSITY OF WALES, ABERYSTWYTH

PATEL TAYLOR, 1998–2001

The University of Wales, Aberystwyth, is a nineteenth-century foundation, originally housed in a Victorian Gothic pile on the seafront. From the 1930s, however, the University College (as it was then known) developed a suburban campus at Penglais, overlooking Cardigan Bay and close to the National Library of Wales. There was a dramatic expansion of the college during the 1960s, with the late Dale Owen of Percy Thomas Partnership as masterplanner. Patel Taylor's television, theatre and film studies block, commissioned as part of the 125th anniversary celebrations of the college, could be seen as a homage to the 1960s: the practice finds much to admire in the Percy Thomas campus.

While in tune with its context the building has a straightforward elegance combined with a clear delight in the qualities of materials, a typical feature of this youthful practice's work. The site is a plateau at a strategic position on the main route through the campus. The building cuts into the hillside and capitalizes on the fine views of the bay.

The brief provided for two principal theatre spaces, plus backstage facilities, rehearsal rooms, editing and recording rooms, and offices. The two theatres, essentially windowless spaces, are placed on either side of the central stepped route, crossed by bridges, that bisects the building. Backstage and technical spaces are placed deep within the building, with rehearsal rooms and the generously sized foyer enjoying the fine views out to the west. The budget was far from extravagant, but the finishes are never poor quality and always practical. The tiles, timber and white plaster of the foyer create an ambience recalling that of the Royal Festival Hall, London, a building that Patel Taylor much admires.

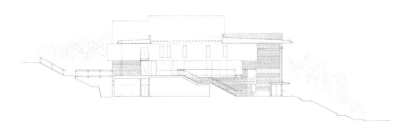

Above and top right
Patel Taylor's addition to the Aberystwyth campus includes a new stepped internal route crossed by bridges.

Right and opposite
Facing west to the sea, the building is part of a largely 1960s campus that was something of an inspiration to its architects.

TRINITY COLLEGE OF MUSIC
GREENWICH, LONDON SE10

JOHN McASLAN & PARTNERS, 1999–2001

Trinity College of Music, one of Britain's leading musical academies, was one of the beneficiaries when the Royal Naval College moved out of the former Royal Hospital in Greenwich. The imposing Baroque complex, begun in 1662 and intended initially as a royal palace but completed as a home for retired seamen, was the work of John Webb, Christopher Wren, Nicholas Hawksmoor and John Vanbrugh; the Royal Naval College took over the site in 1873. Listed Grade I and awarded ancient monument status, the buildings, including some of the finest in Britain, are part of a World Heritage Site.

With 600 students formerly housed in a number of buildings in central London, Trinity College was allocated the King Charles Building, the first of the blocks at Greenwich to be begun (by Webb) but only completed well into the eighteenth century. The Royal Hospital includes several magnificent interiors, notably the Painted Hall and a chapel, but most of the blocks contained utilitarian accommodation for aged seafarers. Over the last century most of the original fit-out had been removed, opening the way for the stripping out of later partitions to create rehearsal rooms, offices, a library and social spaces.

Given a relatively modest budget – £7,750,000 for 7500 square metres (80,730 square feet) – the project had to be matter of fact, with few trimmings. Services are generally left frankly exposed and surface-mounted. Ventilation is provided simply by opening windows. The skeleton of the building is able to withstand the heavy wear it will inevitably sustain. The juxtaposition of the old structure with new interventions is one of the most satisfying aspects of reuse projects such as this: at Greenwich it is seen to good effect in the top-floor Jerwood Library, where the great timber roof trusses have been left open to view.

There is a sense in this project of Trinity College simply inhabiting the historic building – conversion has not taken place. This is appropriate for the Greenwich site because it has already been through several changes of function, and the music students may not be there forever. However, McAslan has drawn up plans for a second, more ambitious phase of development in which the central court of the building would be covered with a glazed roof, giving the college a large sheltered social and performance space. This proposal waits on funding and the necessary consents.

Right
Trinity College is housed in part of the finest complex of Baroque buildings in Britain.

Opposite
The conversion was both economical and respectful to the historic interiors: in the top-floor library, magnificent oak trusses have been opened up to view.

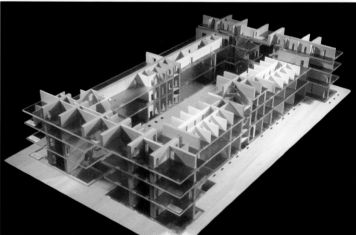

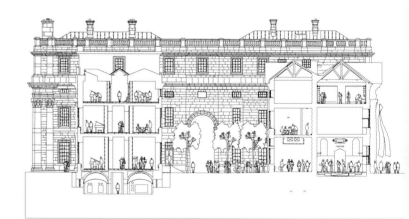

CLOTH HALL STREET DEVELOPMENT
LEEDS, WEST YORKSHIRE
ALLFORD HALL MONAGHAN MORRIS

CORINTHIAN VILLA AND REGENCY VILLA
REGENT'S PARK, LONDON NW1
ERITH & TERRY ARCHITECTS

No 1 DEANSGATE AND URBIS, MANCHESTER
IAN SIMPSON ARCHITECTS

DIRTY HOUSE, WHITECHAPEL, LONDON E1
ADJAYE ASSOCIATES

DROP HOUSE, FIRS WOOD CLOSE, NORTHAW
HERTFORDSHIRE
HUDSON FEATHERSTONE

DUNCAN HOUSE, KINLOCH, FIFE
GARETH HOSKINS ARCHITECTS

FAITH HOUSE, HOLTON LEE CENTRE
POOLE, DORSET
TONY FRETTON ARCHITECTS

GARNER STREET HOUSE, BETHNAL GREEN
LONDON E2
FAT

GRAFTON NEW HALL, GRAFTON HALL ESTATE
CHESHIRE
USHIDA FINDLAY

HILL HOUSE, HAMPSTEAD, LONDON NW3
AVANTI ARCHITECTS

HOLLICK HOUSE, MANOR FARM, HADDENHAM
BUCKINGHAMSHIRE
PROCTOR MATTHEWS

KNIGHT HOUSE
RICHMOND UPON THAMES, SURREY
DAVID CHIPPERFIELD ARCHITECTS

MILLENNIUM VILLAGE, GREENWICH PENINSULA
LONDON SE10
ERSKINE TOVATT/EPR

THE MOAT HOUSE, DORSINGTON
NR STRATFORD-UPON-AVON, WARWICKSHIRE
GLENN HOWELLS ARCHITECTS

PHELAN BARKER HOUSE, TOLLESBURY, ESSEX
BUSCHOW HENLEY

POOLHOUSE, SOUTH-EAST ENGLAND
USHIDA FINDLAY

POTTERS' FIELDS HOUSING, SOUTHWARK
LONDON SE1
IAN RITCHIE ARCHITECTS

PRIVATE HOUSE, HERTFORDSHIRE
FRASER BROWN McKENNA ARCHITECTS

QUAKER BARNS, HAVERINGLAND, NORFOLK
HUDSON ARCHITECTS

TALL HOUSE, ARTHUR ROAD, WIMBLEDON
LONDON SW19
TERRY PAWSON

TIMBER WHARF HOUSING, MANCHESTER
GLENN HOWELLS ARCHITECTS

VXO HOUSE, SPANIARDS END, HAMPSTEAD
LONDON NW3
ALISON BROOKS ARCHITECTS

CLOTH HALL STREET DEVELOPMENT
LEEDS, WEST YORKSHIRE

ALLFORD HALL MONAGHAN MORRIS, 2000–04

The mixed-use scheme fills a gap site adjacent to the Grade I-listed Corn Exchange and uses a local palette of materials, including brick and glazed faience.

This £6,500,000 project for a commercial and residential development was won as the result of a limited design competition run by the client, Welfield Ltd, and its architectural advisers for a large vacant site lying within a conservation area in the centre of Leeds. From previous planning applications for the site it was clear that the planners were looking for a contemporary approach that respected but did not ape the largely Victorian architecture of the surrounding area. There has been much local interest in the progress of the design. The project has been notable for the proactive support given by the planners and the city architect, as well as constructive comment from the Civic Trust and Leeds Architectural Initiative.

The development lies within the Exchange Quarter of Leeds, noted for its vibrant mix of new bars, restaurants and specialist shops. The site is bounded by Cloth Hall Street, Crown Street, Call Lane and the railway viaduct adjacent to Assembly Street.

The building falls within a conservation area. Immediately adjacent are the Grade I-listed Corn Exchange, which has been recently converted into shops, and the remaining elements of the Grade II-listed White Cloth Hall, recently converted into a restaurant. This project is unashamedly modern, but draws inspiration from the Victorian warehouses still prevalent in the area and from the faience decoration of the shopping arcades.

Four storeys containing fifty-seven apartments wrap around the triangular site to form a courtyard at first-floor level, above retail units at ground and basement levels. The courtyard serves as a private space, with external access walkways to each apartment. The building is set back from the railway viaduct to allow for an extension of Assembly Street, to provide for vehicular service access and convivial use of the space for the ground-floor bar.

The apartments have been designed with generous ceiling heights and large windows to give the spacious feel of a converted warehouse rarely provided in speculative new-build housing. The typical apartment arrangement on the first, second and third floors has been designed to minimize the need for enclosed escape corridors by including alternative means of escape through the second bedroom to the courtyard access deck. The plan is, therefore, cleanly divided into bedrooms on one side and living accommodation on the other. The fourth floor has larger penthouse apartments with full-height, set-back glazing at front and back.

The three external faces of the scheme reflect their immediate contexts. First, the Cloth Hall Street elevation is concave in plan, acknowledging the curvature of the robust Corn Exchange opposite. The façade is composed of a regular grid of Victorian pressed brick and a chequerboard pattern of large clear windows with faience panels of graduated colours. The formal window pattern reflects the arrangement of apartments floor by floor, with the ceramic panel corresponding to the position of each bedroom. This arrangement has been emphasized further by the use of flat steel frames lining the large window-opening brick reveals, in contrast to the revealed thickness of the brick bedroom openings and ceramic panels. Secondly, the Call Lane elevation resolves the 'stitching together' of the modern form of the Corn Exchange façade with the existing Victorian buildings at nos. 27–33 Call Lane. Thirdly, the elevation facing the railway viaduct and the Calls area of Leeds begins to break the formality of the Cloth Hall Street elevation by the expression of the faience panels as sliding planes.

The shopfront base of the building extends the language of the façade above and slightly inverts it. However, there is a clear separation between the base and upper levels by the white back-lit glass signage band around the building.

CORINTHIAN VILLA AND REGENCY VILLA
REGENT'S PARK, LONDON NW1

ERITH & TERRY ARCHITECTS, 1989–2003

Quinlan Terry's commission from the Crown Estate to design six new villas on the north-western edge of Regent's Park, London, was, he recalls, like "being asked to step into John Nash's shoes and keep on walking". In the early nineteenth century Nash had planned to build up to fifty villas in the park, which he 'improved' for the Prince Regent (later George IV), one of the greatest and most imaginative patrons of architecture in British history. Few of these were actually built; instead, a series of grand terraces was constructed around the perimeter of the park.

The site for the new houses was obtained by demolishing some inter-war residential blocks belonging to the former Bedford College. Terry conceived the development as a three-dimensional history of the Classical tradition, which he considers to be the source of all 'civilized' architecture. By 1991 three houses had been built; one of them, the Gothick Villa, is a reflection of the perennial fascination of

Classical architects with the medieval. The economic recession of the 1990s brought the project to a temporary halt. It was revived by a developer, who was required to work within strict covenants laid down by the Crown Estate, with the last of the houses completed in 2003. Of the final group, the Corinthian Villa, with its curved façade inspired by the Baroque architect Francesco Borromini, is the most striking.

All of the houses are finely crafted, with high-quality details realized in appropriate materials. They have found a ready market among London's super-rich, although their interiors, apart from the grand staircases (which are something of a Terry hallmark), are far from grandiose. The façades – the most distinctive features – can be seen by anyone walking along the park's Outer Circle (and doubtless being watched on camera, as the American ambassador's residence is across the road). They form one of the most extraordinary confections in the recent architectural history of London.

The six villas at Regent's Park provide an extraordinary potted history of the Classical tradition.

No. 1 DEANSGATE AND URBIS, MANCHESTER
IAN SIMPSON ARCHITECTS, 1996–2002

Ian Simpson's apartment building at No. 1 Deansgate in Manchester is a short walk away from his 1998 Urbis building. Largely funded by the Millennium Commission, Urbis is the most dramatic new building to emerge from the reconstruction of central Manchester that followed the 1996 IRA bombing. Clad in frameless glazing, its dynamic form gives the city an instant new landmark, and the project has helped to reconnect the long-rundown area around Manchester Cathedral and Victoria station into the central core of the city. The problem with Urbis, however, as with other National Lottery projects before it, seems to lie in a lack of clearly defined purpose.

In contrast, Simpson's No. 1 Deansgate is a project driven by the market and built by one of the largest residential developers, Crosby Homes. The scheme was previewed in the masterplan (on which Simpson worked) for the Millennium Quarter drawn up in the aftermath of the bombing, which provided for a residential element alongside the dominant retailing development. At first, the site looks like a left-over, shoved hard up against traffic-laden Deansgate. Simpson, however, addressed the challenge of the location with real panache: it is the building's uncompromising stance and sheer street-cred that grabs attention. The big steel struts cantilevering out from the two-storey retail base are as expressive as they are functional. A generous double-height reception lobby for the eighty-four apartments (virtually all sold off-plan) sits above the shops.

Living right on the city streets means coping with noise and fumes. Simpson addressed this issue by ringing the building with a buffer zone 1.7 metres (5½ feet) wide, glazed with adjustable opening louvres, beyond the double-glazed skin of the apartments. This is really a habitable private balcony space – open balconies would not be practical in this location – which insulates the building against noise and helps to reduce energy consumption.

Opposite
The dramatic glazed form of Urbis houses an exhibition devoted to the history of cities and urban life.

Above
No. 1 Deansgate is an example of how speculative housing can be used to regenerate a city. The double-glazed skin provides a calm living environment in the middle of the frenetic commercial heart of Manchester.

DIRTY HOUSE, WHITECHAPEL, LONDON E1

ADJAYE ASSOCIATES, 2001–02

Opposite
The Dirty House presents an enigmatic, even anonymous, façade to the East End street in which it stands.

Below
The interior makes skilful use of toplighting, while an external terrace offers views across the City of London.

David Adjaye's Elektra House in Whitechapel, east London, completed in 2000, created something of a furore: its entirely blank street façade was criticized as an antisocial, defensive gesture. But the form of the house was both a response to a deprived area and a reflection of the needs of the occupants.

The enigmatically named Dirty House, located in the same area, is an equally unsettling design, eschewing conventional notions of domestic ease. Like the Elektra House it is intended as a live/work space (for artists Tim Noble and Sue Webster). The house is basically a conversion of a plain 1930s warehouse. The internal

structure was removed, in consultation with engineer Techniker, to make two double-height studios that occupy most of the ground and first floors. A new residential pavilion, fully glazed, sits on the roof, its own roof cantilevering out to cover an external terrace; lighting fitted under the timber decking makes this part of the building appear as a dramatic light beam by night. The setting back of the pavilion ensures complete privacy. The main street façades have been covered in anti-graffiti paint and fitted with double-glazed mirror-glass windows, so that from the outside the house appears impenetrable and disturbingly anonymous. There is an air

of menace, too, in the very narrow, two-storey-high hallway through which the house is entered.

Like John Soane, Adjaye uses architectural form to create strong emotional responses: his is an architecture of sensation rather than conventional aesthetics, and compression is a device he uses to powerful effect. Adjaye's skilful use of toplighting is equally Soanean. However, as a modern architect for whom Soane's Classical inheritance is meaningless, Adjaye eschews elaborate detail in favour of a virtuoso approach to the use of materials – whether costly or, like those in this house, essentially commonplace.

DROP HOUSE, FIRS WOOD CLOSE
NORTHAW, HERTFORDSHIRE

HUDSON FEATHERSTONE, 1997–2001

Standing out smooth and white from its context of neo-Tudor and neo-Georgian villas, Drop House, designed by the former partnership of Anthony Hudson and Sarah Featherstone, looks like a throwback to the 1930s. It is refreshing to learn that the house aroused as much opposition from some of the neighbours as a design by Berthold Lubetkin or Connell, Ward & Lucas might have done seventy years ago. The influence on Drop House of the classic era of Modernism and, in particular, of Le Corbusier's Villa Savoye at Poissy-sur-Seine is clear and acknowledged. Yet this is no re-run of historic Modern Movement themes; Drop House is rich in those typically Post-modern qualities of irony, subversion and humour and very far from purist. Indeed, it is its eclecticism that marks it out most clearly as a product of the last decade of the twentieth century.

The house, built for a professional couple, occupies one of five plots where new houses have been developed backing on to established woodland. In contrast to its neighbours, Drop House is pushed to the back of the sloping site to take maximum advantage of light and views to the south across the garden. The inevitably shady, north-facing back garden is small,

and the house reaches out to the trees beyond.

The 'drop' in Drop House is apparent as you approach the house from the front: a giant egg dropped into the orthogonal frame and emerging as a little dome at roof level. At the main living level – the undercroft contains guest accommodation and storage rather than a Corbusian void – it houses a utility room leading off the kitchen. Above, it contains the main bathroom: it is an allegorical as much as a practical device, expressing the 'wet' spaces in the house. The drop helps to break down the formal order of the interior; this is no ideal villa, rather an imaginative response to the specific needs of the users. Nor is there anything purist or minimalist about the choice of materials: acrylic-coated timber panels, artificial stone blocks, travertine marble, even purple leather are among the internal finishes. Spatially, too, the house eschews rational geometry in favour of dramatic effects and highly individual spaces for the clients and their family. Drop House is a place of unexpected vistas and visual surprises, but it did not win a Royal Institute of British Architects Award, for all its obvious quality. Its irreverence and unpredictability may well shock the sober-minded.

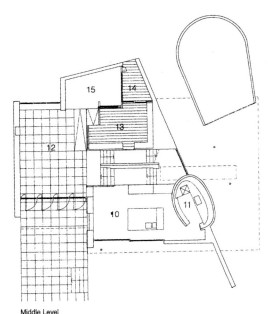

Middle Level
10 Kitchen
11 Utility
12 Living Room
13 Study
14 Study Terrace
15 AV Room

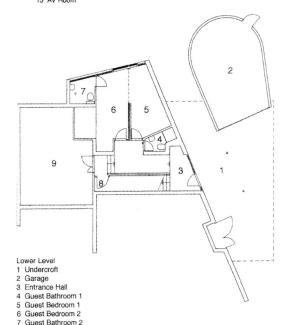

Lower Level
1 Undercroft
2 Garage
3 Entrance Hall
4 Guest Bathroom 1
5 Guest Bedroom 1
6 Guest Bedroom 2
7 Guest Bathroom 2
8 Store
9 Main Store

Right
Although drawing inspiration from the classic villas of the Modern Movement, Drop House has a fluid and radical plan that is typically late twentieth century in character.

Opposite
While referring explicitly to Le Corbusier's Villa Savoye, the house subverts its formal geometry and uses materials of an unconventional nature, for example reconstituted stone.

DUNCAN HOUSE, KINLOCH, FIFE

GARETH HOSKINS ARCHITECTS, 2000–02

Scotland can boast some exciting recent examples of high-quality modern design inserted into historic settings: Jamie Troughton and Hugh Broughton's shop and restaurant at Blair Castle, and Munkenbeck & Marshall's visitor centre on the Isle of Bute (see pp. 72–73) are examples. Gareth Hoskins's Duncan House at Kinloch is sited in a listed walled garden, adjacent to a country house. The new building responds to the geometry of the garden enclosure in an entirely modern way. The experience of living in the house is characterized by the overlapping of internal and external spaces.

The house is defined by two masonry walls, one of which cuts through the garden wall to lead into a small entrance court and an elliptical timber music-room that marks the entry to the house itself. The second wall runs at right angles to the other wall along the central path through the garden, and screens the bedrooms and bathrooms. The main living spaces sit in the angle of the two walls, facing south to the garden. These spaces are fully glazed with frameless glazing, and are stepped back below a boldly oversailing roof to create areas of different heights. Full-height timber doors can be opened in fine weather to allow free movement between house and garden.

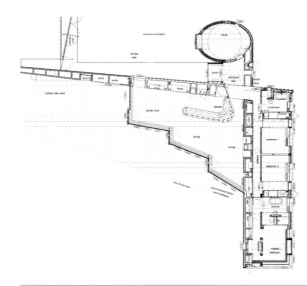

east elevation

west elevation

Above
The house is located in a walled garden; its form responds to the enclosed space.

Right and opposite
The main living spaces are fully glazed but set back beneath an oversailing roof that provides shelter from the unpredictable Scottish weather.

FAITH HOUSE, HOLTON LEE CENTRE
POOLE, DORSET

TONY FRETTON ARCHITECTS, 1999–2002

Tony Fretton is an architect whose close involvement with working artists infuses his approach to the design of buildings for the visual and performing arts. Not for Fretton is a building a neutral container: his work on London's Lisson Gallery involved consultations with the artists Julian Opie, Tony Cragg, Anish Kapoor and Richard Deacon. Fretton's buildings have a quality of deliberate 'ordinariness' that contrasts with the 'temple of art' approach that sets art apart from everyday life: his architecture can be seen instead as a continuing dialogue between art and life.

The Holton Lee Centre in Dorset was established by a charitable trust working with the disabled "in the areas of personal growth, the arts, the natural environment and non-denominational spirituality". (Alex

Sainsbury, who commissioned a house from Fretton in Chelsea, London, is one of the trustees.) The centre was based initially in a group of converted farm buildings, with a new-build hostel block added in the late 1990s. Fretton was commissioned to design a block of artists' studios, a building containing archives and research facilities, and another multi-purpose building to be used as chapel, meeting-room and gallery. The last, named Faith House, was the first building to be completed. Constructed for just £150,000, it contains a large meeting-room, smaller 'quiet room', lobby space with small kitchen, and WCs.

In seeking an appropriate language for a contemporary religious building unencumbered by the imagery of a particular faith, Fretton was clearly influenced by

Gunnar Asplund's Stockholm Crematorium in Sweden (completed in 1940), which itself looks to the tradition of the Classical temple. Four timber columns support the entrance canopy. The basic structure is entirely timber, with unpainted cedar cladding (intended to weather to a silver hue) and a layer of soil on the flat roof. The quiet room features a ring of birch trunks enclosing the central space and symbolizing the Holton Lee philosophy of harmony with nature. A full-height window provides views of the fields and heathland outside. The building could not be more straightforward: its simplicity seems almost contrived. Yet it has a real spiritual quality all too lacking in most of the new conventional religious buildings of recent years.

Fretton's Faith House seeks to embrace the landscape while providing a calm space for prayer and contemplation.

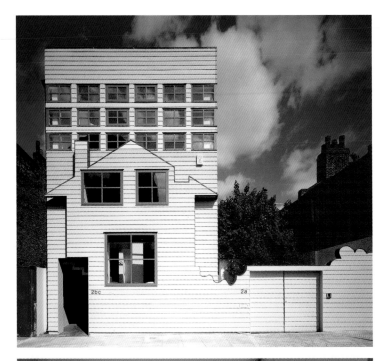

FAT (standing for Fashion, Architecture and Taste) is a design collaborative accustomed to infringing the rules of 'good' taste, so you would expect a house designed by partner Sean Griffiths for his own occupation to be anything but conventional. In fact, Griffiths's house at Garner Street, Bethnal Green, is deliberately populist and pop, designed to communicate with the surrounding community. It opens up to the gritty streets of the East End as if they were located in some gentrified seaport in New England.

The American theme is to the fore here. American Post-modernism has always generated hostility in Britain, being seen as reactionary, trite and lacking in seriousness, and the work of Robert Venturi (responsible for the admittedly lacklustre Sainsbury Wing at The National Gallery, London) has been singled out for special condemnation. Venturi's work is the first comparison that springs to mind when you see the extraordinary street elevation of the Garner Street House. This consists of a cut-out house front, complete with chimney and garden hedge, standing in front of a cut-out office-block façade. Along the side elevation the roofline is decorated with cut-out gables imitating those in Amsterdam. The whole edifice is clad in clapboard, painted sky blue.

The plan of the house too owes something to Venturi/Scott Brown, with a staircase that wraps around the front of the house, creating a double façade, and embraces the kitchen inglenook. Griffiths, however, describes his creation as "Adolf Loos meets South Park ... . It is deliberately cartoon-like and representational in appearance and its 'pop' references seek to communicate with a wide audience."

The house includes both an office area and a separate top-floor flat, both accessed directly from the street. The house itself is entered from the yard at the side. The kitchen/dining-room is the heart of the house, with bedrooms on two floors above. Apart from Anglo-American PoMo and Pop, the pervasive influence seems to be that of the Arts and Crafts Movement: some of the detail refers explicitly to the Arts and Crafts architect and designer Charles Voysey. Strong colours are used throughout. All in all, it is hugely out of step with its environs. Griffiths denies that the house is in any way flippant, yet its obvious wit and lack of guile are attractive. This is one of the oddest and most memorable London houses since Piers Gough's residence, completed in 1988, for the journalist Janet Street-Porter in Clerkenwell, London.

FAT's Garner Street House externally makes obvious reference to the pop imagery of Post-modernism (*top*), but internally combines free-flowing contemporary space with Art and Crafts-inspired details (*middle and bottom*).

GRAFTON NEW HALL
GRAFTON HALL ESTATE, CHESHIRE

USHIDA FINDLAY, 2001–

Claimed as a radical reincarnation of the English country house, Grafton New Hall incorporates not only twenty-first-century amenities, but also a low-energy services programme that uses natural light and the insulative qualities of the soil.

The English country house is generally associated with a culture of continuity and, indeed, conservatism. Since the Second World War architecturally significant new houses in the countryside have been the preserve of such traditionalist architects as Raymond Erith, Francis Johnson, Quinlan Terry and Robert Adam.

Grafton New Hall is an attempt to break this mould and create "a twenty-first-century vision for country living". The site has been inhabited since medieval times and was formerly occupied by the old Grafton Hall, demolished in 1963. In 2001 a limited competition was organized by developer Ferrario Burns Hood for a new house on the site. While current planning policies generally rule out the building of new single large houses in rural areas, an exception can be made where "a truly outstanding" design is submitted. Ushida Findlay's winning scheme duly received full planning consent in 2002, and the architects then went in search of an affluent patron with around £10,000,000 to spare on a new house. Set in the Manchester commuter belt, it is calculated to appeal to the big spenders who have fuelled the city's retail, restaurant and property boom. This is a luxury home – 3500 square metres (37,670 square feet) in size – with every amenity, including a cinema, two swimming-pools, a gym and an art gallery.

The form of the house is distinctly organic, a spreading, low-rise structure erupting from the soil like a monster in science fiction. The architects compare it to "a series of ridges and furrows which reflect, enhance and frame the natural contours of the medieval landscape". The accommodation is spread through a series of wings, all of which benefit from generous natural light: the house is designed, it is claimed, for low-energy living in tune with nature – not that a potential buyer is likely to need to worry much about fuel bills.

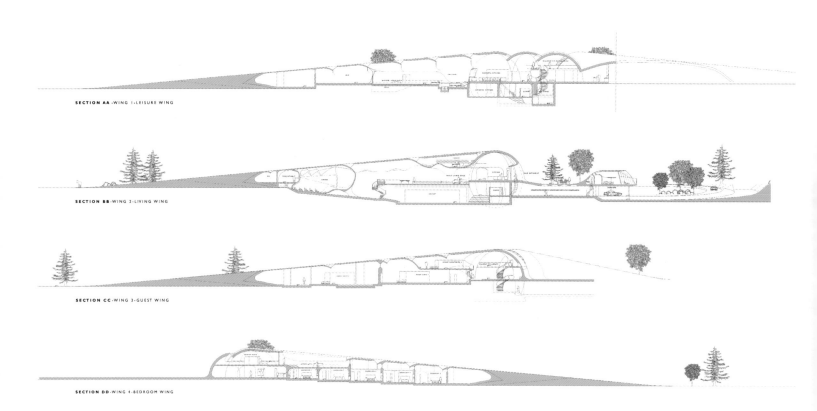

SECTION AA · WING 1 · LEISURE WING

SECTION BB · WING 2 · LIVING WING

SECTION CC · WING 3 · GUEST WING

SECTION DD · WING 4 · BEDROOM WING

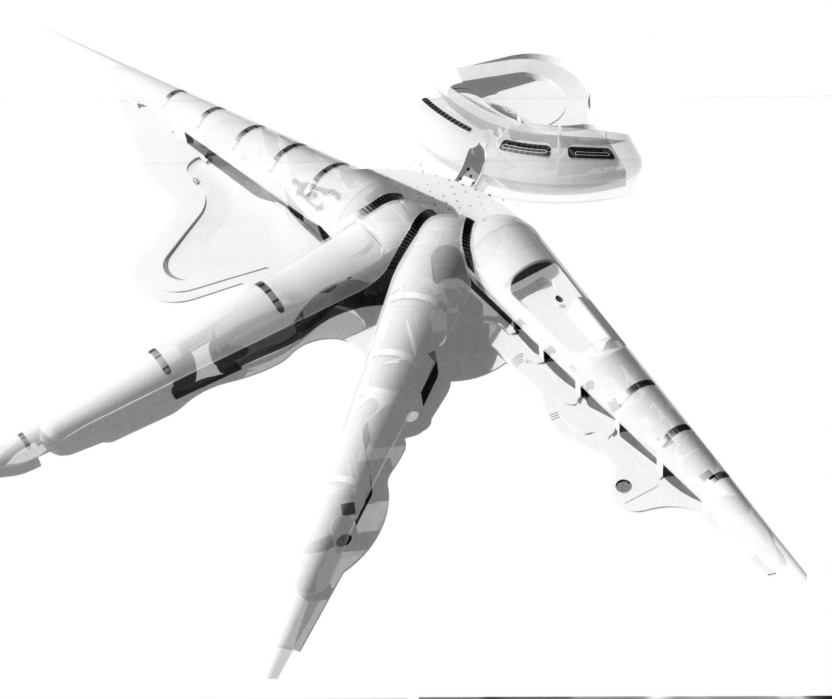

HILL HOUSE, HAMPSTEAD, LONDON NW3
AVANTI ARCHITECTS, 1998–2001

John Allan of Avanti Architects is not only a major writer on the Modern Movement (with two books on Berthold Lubetkin's work), but he is also an acknowledged authority on the repair of Modern Movement buildings: Lubetkin's Penguin Pool at London Zoo, Goldfinger's house in Willow Road, Hampstead, Connell, Ward & Lucas's White House and Patrick Gwynne's The Homewood, both in Surrey, are among the Modernist landmarks he has restored.

At the Hill House, Allan was dealing with a house that, far from being a Modernist icon, was relatively unknown. Designed in 1936, it was the work of Oliver Hill, a fluent architect in the neo-Tudor and Georgian styles whose versatility excluded him from the inner circle of Modernists for whom conviction was all. Yet Hill, when the need arose, could produce as convincing a design in the manner of Le Corbusier or Erich Mendelsohn as most English architects of his day.

The Hill House was, in fact, pioneering in its use of exposed brick as a cladding material, although a number of Modern houses of the 1930s in Britain used rendered brick rather than reinforced concrete (strictly a sham). Many concrete houses of the inter-war period have deteriorated drastically, but Hill's brick weathered well. The Hill House had, however, suffered from radical alterations: original rooms had been subdivided, the main staircase destroyed and a new (and ugly) top storey added.

Elements of strict restoration are less significant than the bold additions designed by Avanti. The new staircase is set in a semicircular bay, part of an extension to the rear of the house that includes a new kitchen. The rooftop extension was demolished and replaced by a new lightweight pavilion, a deliberate contrast to the existing house, which takes advantage of the fine views from the elevated site. Had the house been listed, it is likely that a less radical approach, copying the existing fabric, would have been imposed on the architects. As it stands, the house has become, in the words of critic Alan Powers, "a healthy hybrid".

The reconstruction of Oliver Hill's Hill House involved the removal of incongruous alterations and the addition of a new glazed rooftop pavilion (*above*), a striking contrast to the solid brick façades of the 1930s house.

Opposite
Dramatic double-height spaces are combined
with a skilful use of natural light in the interiors
of Hollick House.

Below
The external form of the house makes clear
reference to the Arts and Crafts tradition in
layout and massing.

Haddenham, near Aylesbury, Buckinghamshire, is noted for its "many worthwhile buildings and picturesque groups", says Pevsner's *The Buildings of England*. The village is of interest to students of post-war architecture for the distinguished additions to its fabric made by Peter Aldington during the 1960s: three thoroughly modern houses, including one for himself (with a wonderful garden), designed to fit unobtrusively into the tight village core. In the 1970s Aldington & Craig converted a former bakery in the village into practice offices. The challenge for a young practice such as Proctor Matthews of working in Haddenham was therefore considerable; Peter Aldington was, in fact, brought in to advise on the selection of an architect for the additions to Manor Farm, the farm complex next to the church.

Manor Farm is of outstanding interest: partly medieval in date, and with a magnificent tithe barn, it is occupied by three generations of the Hollick family. Proctor Matthews's first commission on the site was to convert a small barn and outbuildings for residential use. The new house was a more difficult proposition, involving extended consultations with planners and the local community. Popular taste has not necessarily advanced since the days when Aldington added so successfully to the local scene and there was some pressure for a more 'rural' look. The house forms three sides of a south-facing courtyard, with the full-height living-room and kitchen framing the bedroom wing and connected by a conservatory. The use of simple render, timber boarding and tiled roofs connects the house to the neighbouring farm buildings, although there is no attempt to make it into a fake barn. The interiors are light-filled and open, with no hint of cottagey clutter. The landscape around the house is notable – the client is a landscape designer. Proctor Matthews could hardly ignore the example of Aldington's work in Haddenham; the strength of the project reflects his influence, but its transparency and lightness are entirely contemporary.

KNIGHT HOUSE, RICHMOND UPON THAMES, SURREY

DAVID CHIPPERFIELD ARCHITECTS, 1987–90; EXTENDED 2001

To the existing 1980s house (*below, left and right*), David Chipperfield has added a new pavilion (*below, middle, and opposite*) that contains an office with a bedroom above. The glazed end wall of the bedroom slides down to form an open loggia.

When Chipperfield designed the house at Richmond upon Thames, Surrey, for Nick and Charlotte Knight he was known for domestic work and shop interiors. Fifteen years on, he is undertaking large-scale public commissions in Germany, Spain and Italy, and finally has a substantial project in Britain (see pp. 216–17).

The original Knight House was, in theory, an enlargement and reworking of an existing house set in a typical suburban avenue. In fact, the house was completely transformed so that it was more than doubled in size. The new house, which was highly contentious when built, extends into the rear garden, where a studio space overlooks a courtyard, itself enclosed by a concrete arch. One of its special strengths was the remarkable interaction of internal and external space, with a virtuosity in the management of natural light for which Chipperfield is now renowned. In many respects, this relatively modest house was one of the key British buildings of the 1980s. The 2001 extension was constructed on the site of a neighbouring house, acquired by the Knights and demolished. With its pitched, slate-covered roof (demanded by planners), it has an identity of its own, in tune with the ingrained individualism of the suburbs (where every plot is a separate domain). The extension provides an office and archive store at ground level, with a large bedroom above. A small link block, containing cloakrooms and a bathroom, connects new and existing elements; a small courtyard is formed between the two.

The diagram of the extension is as incisive and perfectly judged as you would expect from Chipperfield. The use of materials equally reflects the touch of a master. The beautifully constructed timber stair connecting the two floors is an exquisite thing in itself. Chipperfield's architecture is sometimes seen as a matter of control and refinement, but he enjoys dramatic gestures. The glazed end wall of the Knights' bedroom slides down into a slot in the floor, turning the whole room into an open loggia. The Knight House reflects admirably that quality described by one Italian critic as *un sensibile minimalismo*.

MILLENNIUM VILLAGE
GREENWICH PENINSULA, LONDON SE10
ERSKINE TOVATT/EPR, 1997–

The 1997 competition for the development of the Millennium Village, a short distance from the Millennium Dome, was won by Greenwich Millennium Village Ltd, working with the veteran Anglo-Swedish architect Ralph Erskine (in the context of a Richard Rogers masterplan for the peninsula). The designs have been developed and carried through to construction by Erskine's office in collaboration with the British EPR practice.

Erskine is best known in Britain for the famous Byker Wall, Newcastle upon Tyne, where the long-established local community, earmarked for rehousing, was involved in the design of the new 1400-unit development. As at Byker, but in a very different context (the community at Greenwich is newly formed), the Erskine team sought to instil the new housing with something of the sense of place and identity found in traditional urban settlements. The village contains a mix of uses and social classes: 'affordable' housing is scattered through the scheme. Some of the housing is by other hands (for example, the excellent 189-unit development completed by Proctor Matthews in 2001), while the equally outstanding school and community centre are by Edward Cullinan Architects.

As development proceeds, the idea of a 'village' begins to emerge as something more than wishful thinking. The masterplan, with its green 'eco-park' and central Oval, with retail and office development, is well considered. The housing itself is strong in form (and makes bold use of colour), but is tough and unprecious enough to survive the attentions of project managers and contractors and to lend itself to the use of prefabricated components. Within the overall framework there is scope for a number of housing types; Erskine was, after all, a member of Team X, and its dislike of the universal and the prescriptive has always characterized his work. Balconies, bays, varied claddings and other devices break down the uniformity of the blocks, which are tallest at the north-east edge of the site, close to the River Thames. High environmental standards are fundamental to the project: grey water is recycled and rainwater collected. Recycled materials have been extensively used and insulation values are high.

The saga of the Dome has been sufficiently depressing to cast a blight on the development of the Greenwich peninsula, but too few critics of the former ever bother to visit the site. The long-term success of the Millennium Village remains to be seen, but the evidence so far suggests that it could succeed where most London Docklands housing developments – largely self-contained enclosures detached from their surroundings – have failed.

The dense, socially mixed Millennium Village housing establishes a challenging pattern for the development of brownfield sites.

THE MOAT HOUSE, DORSINGTON
NR STRATFORD-UPON-AVON, WARWICKSHIRE

GLENN HOWELLS ARCHITECTS, 2001–02

Firmly within the Miesian tradition, Glenn Howells's spare addition to the Cotswold stone Moat House reaches out into the surrounding landscape, and cantilevers over the historic moat.

The adaptation of The Moat House, located in a remote part of Warwickshire, was commissioned by a developer client of Glenn Howells Architects as a small-scale private intervention. From an architectural background himself, the client desired an uncompromisingly modern approach. While the brief did not initially define a specific singular function for the space, it has become a highly used living area and reading room, and a display case for the client's collection of art works and furnishings.

The original house dates back in parts to the twelfth century. The site has been adapted on numerous occasions, in part through its use as a collection of farm buildings that serviced the surrounding 34 hectares (85 acres) of land, and more recently through its conversion to a family home and company offices. The linear blocks of the offices and living quarters form two courtyards, in turn surrounded by a number of other formal and informal gardens and landscaped zones, most significantly the original moat, which has provided the dramatic setting for the new structure.

The concise articulation and orientation of the structure capitalizes on the remote context of the house and its surroundings, forming a contrast to both the weight of the existing elevation and the informally landscaped moat edge. Externally the structure appears to be supported by the rough stone wall, which continues the aesthetic of the adjacent landscape and provides a contrasting plinth to the horizontal planes that form the roof and floor. The dark frames to the four sliding openings recede against the glazed elevations.

The intention was to provide a distinct contrast to the low and dark interior of the original house. The use of glass-to-glass joints in all locations; the integration of the framing into the roof, floor and existing stone elevation; the light, neutral soffit; and the provision of generous openings create a neutrality that allows the distant and immediate natural environment to dominate the space. The honed limestone flooring was chosen to complement the local Horton stone, and provides a visually rich surface that references the surrounding hard landscaping.

Cantilevered over the moat, the structure is balanced by a series of compression and tension piles, which avoids the need to bear on the house's existing foundations (recently underpinned) and elevation. Four rectangular columns set back from the glazing line represent the only visible structural members, the result of a detailed design period in association with the structural engineer.

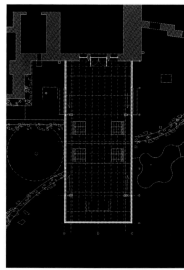

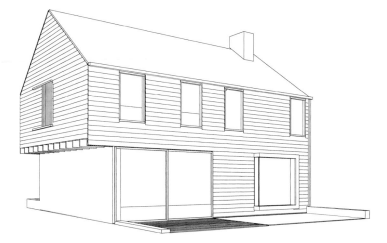

PHELAN BARKER HOUSE, TOLLESBURY, ESSEX

BUSCHOW HENLEY, 2000–01

East Anglia was the homeland of the New Brutalism in the 1950s and 1960s – the Smithsons' Hunstanton School was the defining monument of the movement, and it was in Essex that Nigel Henderson, the *eminence grise* of New Brutalism, came to live in the mid-1950s. Buschow Henley's Phelan Barker House recalls, however, not Hunstanton but the Smithsons' Sugden House, which superficially resembles a typical brick-built, pitch-roofed house of its day. Matter-of-factness is the name of the game, and the same is true of the Phelan Barker House.

The site was a gap at the end of a very ordinary terrace of Victorian brick cottages. The budget was modest, but the client wanted a living space far removed from the compartmented clutter of the nineteenth century. At first sight, the house is deferential to its context, with brick façades and a slate roof. The I-beam that supports the projecting upper storey, however, is a clear reference to Hunstanton. The exposed gable end is weather-boarded, in the local vernacular tradition.

The 'as found' idea pervades the interior, too: the blockwork chimney breast is left exposed, upstairs and down. The ground floor is completely open-plan. Upstairs, three small bedrooms open off a large communal space, enclosed by demountable partitions; only the bathroom is a fixture. The house was built without the supervision of the architects and there are marked imperfections – but perhaps that is part of the story?

Superficially a polite addition to an established street, the Phelan Barker House is externally a commentary on the vernacular tradition, while the interior is largely open-plan with demountable partitions.

POOLHOUSE, SOUTH-EAST ENGLAND

USHIDA FINDLAY, 2000–01

Built for an affluent, security-conscious client – hence the non-specific location – the Poolhouse is an addition to an existing Grade II-listed house standing in a Gertrude Jekyll garden. It is quite simply a container for a 14 x 6-metre (46 x 20-foot) swimming-pool.

Kathryn Findlay went to Japan on a scholarship in 1980 and in 1987 founded the Ushida Findlay practice with her former partner Eisaku Ushida. She returned to Britain in 1997 but the influence of Japan on her work remains strong. At first glance this building is a reference to the English vernacular tradition. The thatched roof – its most distinctive feature – is, however, inspired more by the Japanese art of thatching, *shibamune.* In the Japanese tradition, the broad ridge of a thatched roof is planted; the Poolhouse has a broad ridge, but instead of being entirely planted it contains a rooflight, flooding the interior with daylight, surrounded by planting. The thatch is supported not on a traditional structure but on a glulam substructure resting on concrete posts, with the glazing panels fixed to hollow steel sections. The thatched roof, swooping down to head height on the southern (garden) elevation, shades the glazed wall from the sun. To the north, the building is hard up against a handsome stone garden wall.

This sensuous and beautifully crafted building challenges our preconceptions of tradition and the vernacular. It effortlessly fuses not only old and new technologies, but also two very different cultures.

Below
The Poolhouse merges the thatching traditions of England and Japan to produce a building that is at home in the setting of a classic Jekyll garden.

Opposite
The structure of the building is entirely contemporary using concrete, steel and a roof of glulam timber.

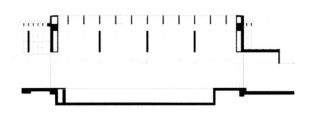

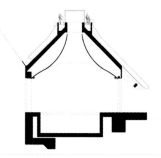

The Potters' Fields housing scheme provides a backcloth to Tower Bridge and the new City Hall, and is seen as a dramatic gateway to Southwark from the City.

POTTERS' FIELDS HOUSING SOUTHWARK, LONDON SE1

IAN RITCHIE ARCHITECTS, 2001–07

The Potters' Fields site has seen several abortive projects in recent years, including a proposed temporary home for the Royal Opera House while its millennium reconstruction was under way, and a housing scheme by Will Alsop. The site is south of Tower Bridge, at the junction of Tower Bridge Road and Tooley Street, and close to an established public park, which is well used but rather bleak. Near by are the regenerated quarter around Shad Thames and the More London development around City Hall, masterplanned by Foster and Partners as an extension of London Bridge City.

Ritchie's client for this scheme is Britain's largest volume house-builder, Berkeley Homes, which seems to be increasingly aware of the power of design as a selling tool. This is a large, dense scheme: 386 apartments (more than a quarter 'affordable'), plus 11,000 square metres (118,000 square feet) of cultural and commercial space on a site of just 1.4 hectares (3.6 acres). The existing Lambeth College building is retained in its present use.

The apartments are arranged in a series of 'mini-towers', eleven to eighteen storeys high and in blocks of four to six storeys along the street line. The tapered, elliptical towers are designed to stand as pavilions in the park, which will be expanded by around 40% as a consequence of the scheme. They are clad in clear and translucent glazing with continuous balconies at every floor level to counter down-draughts. At ground level, new routes are to be created through the site to develop the existing circulation pattern.

In practical terms this scheme, submitted for planning consent early in 2003, looks a winner: the heart of the City is in walking distance (for the energetic) and Southwark is itself developing as a major office quarter. If built, it will be Ritchie's largest work in London and, judging by his superb Jubilee line station at Bermondsey and London Rowing Club in the Royal Docks, something to look forward to.

PRIVATE HOUSE, HERTFORDSHIRE

FRASER BROWN McKENNA ARCHITECTS, 1998–2002

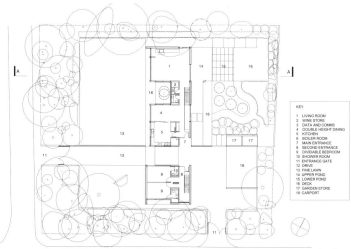

KEY
1 LIVING ROOM
2 WINE STORE
3 DATA AND COMMS
4 DOUBLE HEIGHT DINING
5 KITCHEN
6 BOILER ROOM
7 MAIN ENTRANCE
8 SECOND ENTRANCE
9 DIVIDABLE BEDROOM
10 SHOWER ROOM
11 ENTRANCE GATE
12 DRIVE
13 FINE LAWN
14 UPPER POND
15 LOWER POND
16 DECK
17 GARDEN STORE
18 CARPORT

Ground Floor

For this expensive and beautifully finished house, Fraser Brown McKenna's clients, who are collectors and patrons of the arts, commissioned the practice on the basis of its recent gallery for the Slade School of Art in London. And yet the house is notable not only for the quality of its construction and finishes – it cost £1,200,000 – but equally for its incisive plan and memorable form.

The house replaces an Edwardian villa, the clients' former home, which was demolished, although much of the existing landscape was carefully retained. The two-storey structure contains living and bedroom spaces, including a double-height dining-room, backed by a zone of services and connected by a longitudinal circulation strip on two levels. The drive is taken straight through the house at ground level to access an enclosed, landscaped court with garaging.

Since the clients wished to bring little with them from the old house, Fraser Brown McKenna was given a free hand with new furnishings and fittings, many specially made to the architect's designs. The stairs are covered, unusually, with leather. The interior is the setting for a number of works of art and more are being added. Materials include the extensive use of costly jarrah wood, imported from sustainable sources in Australia, it is claimed, and used internally and externally. Its rich texture is offset by exposed concrete and plain render. From the garden, the strongly expressed fair-faced concrete frame, enclosing full-height glazing, has a powerful impact recalling that of the classic 'white' houses of the 1930s. External louvres and roller blinds inside provide shading on sunny days. There is none of the earnestness of the Modern Movement in this sybaritic house, but its sheer elegance and consistency cannot fail to impress.

The rigorous longitudinal plan of the house (*above and opposite*), which occupies the site of a former Edwardian villa, contrasts with the unashamed opulence of the materials and fit-out, which includes a staircase clad in leather (*right*).

QUAKER BARNS, HAVERINGLAND, NORFOLK

HUDSON ARCHITECTS, 2000–01

Anthony Hudson, formerly in partnership with Sarah Featherstone (see Drop House, pp. 160–61), has maintained his family home in Norfolk through some years of London practice. In this project, he addressed one of the most difficult issues affecting the rural 'heritage': the future of farm buildings. Modern farming has little use for historic barns and other structures, but conversion for residential use too often trivializes and domesticates these impressive structures.

The raw material for this conversion scheme was a cart shed and grain storage barn, part of a complex of buildings already largely converted and close to an occupied farmhouse. The aim was to minimize alterations, particularly to the exteriors of the buildings, and to maintain their robust character. The conversion is low-cost, with a stress on sustainability: most materials used were locally sourced.

Elevations were kept simple, with green-oak cladding at upper level and straw-bale infills in what were once open voids. Window openings are concentrated on the south side, set in simple steel frames sealed with car-window seals, a cheap but effective device. Glass pantiles set into the clay pantile roofs allow light to penetrate the interiors. Inside, flint and brick masonry has been left exposed to offset the impact of new insertions.

Right
Low-cost materials, including the use of steel-framed windows, are a key feature of this project.

Opposite
The fundamental idea of the scheme has been to retain the robust character of the barn while introducing new uses to give the building an extended life.

TALL HOUSE, ARTHUR ROAD
WIMBLEDON, LONDON SW19

TERRY PAWSON, 1996–2002

Houses designed by architects for themselves arguably form a genre in their own right, although it is interesting that many of the biggest names in British architecture – James Stirling, the Smithsons, Rogers and Foster, for example – have opted for adaptations of existing buildings as their London homes. One of the modern classics of London is, however, the elegant 1960s steel house near Wimbledon Common that Richard Rogers designed for his parents. Terry Pawson's house is about 1.5 kilometres (1 mile) away, in an avenue of prosperous Edwardian villas close to Wimbledon Park station.

While the Rogers house, case-study inspired, exemplifies the universalism of the High-tech tradition – it would be at home in Malibu – the Pawson house is more complex, a response to site and context and subtly inspired by history. Pawson cites the nineteenth-century English architect Sir John Soane as one of his greatest inspirations; Soane's influence is reflected in the spatial qualities of the house and its skilful use of toplighting. Architects Louis Kahn and Tadao Ando are other influences, but all are comfortably subsumed into what is a mature and considered work.

The site of the house is extremely narrow and falls away steeply from the road. The section is the key. The principal living spaces are contained in a two-storey, barrel-vaulted concrete pavilion that steps down the slope to the garden. The bedrooms and bathrooms are placed in a four-storey tower, timber-framed (and timber-clad, using unseasoned oak) and facing the road. A full-height staircase hall, top-lit, connects these two elements and is an ideal space for the display of art works. The house is an assembly of pieces in the tradition of James Stirling. Its interior character is formed by contrasting textures: exposed concrete and finely crafted timber floors, and built-in furniture.

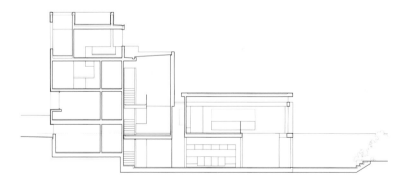

Opposite and top left
Bedrooms and bathrooms are placed in a four-storey tower – containing a dramatic, even perilous, staircase – facing the road.

Bottom left and above
The principal living spaces are housed in a low-rise wing to the rear, facing the garden.

The glazed envelope of the Timber Wharf project provides a calm environment for living and working on a canalside site in central Manchester.

TIMBER WHARF HOUSING, MANCHESTER
GLENN HOWELLS ARCHITECTS, 1998–2002

The Timber Wharf site, close to the Bridgewater canal in the heart of Manchester, is near earlier projects completed by developer Urban Splash, including Britannia Mills and the Box Works. The result is a classic example of regeneration in what was an area of derelict industry.

With the Urban Task Force, chaired by Richard Rogers, already preparing its report to the government, Urban Splash was determined to make the Timber Wharf project a model for new-build schemes on brownfield urban sites. In 1998 an international open competition was launched, with Rogers as one of the judges and a commitment by Urban Splash to construct the winning scheme. Glenn Howells Architects was appointed in April 1999, and construction took place in 2000–02.

The winning scheme, with 180 apartments, was designed with fast-track, low-cost modular construction in mind. The architects' experience of using high-quality precast concrete on previous schemes in Armagh (see pp. 112–13) and Hereford informed the development of the structure, which is rational and robust, generating the strong form and clear identity of the completed development. A fair-faced concrete crosswall system is wrapped in a fully glazed envelope containing a variety of residential spaces, including live/work units. The aim was to reflect the prevalent industrial aesthetic of the neighbourhood and to avoid a vocabulary specifically associated with housing. Duplex units at ground-floor level are designed to be usable as housing or as shops or offices. Garden and courtyard areas along the canalside provide a calm oasis close to the centre of one of Britain's largest conurbations.

Richard Rogers predicted in 1999 that the scheme "will quickly be realized as a design classic". This has turned out to be an astute comment on a project that has important lessons for the ongoing renaissance of the inner city.

VXO HOUSE, SPANIARDS END
HAMPSTEAD, LONDON NW3

ALISON BROOKS ARCHITECTS, 1999–2001

Alison Brooks's VXO House is basically a reworking of an unremarkable house of the 1960s. Hamfistedly extended during the 1970s – space was gained at the expense of convenience and legibility – it now forms the core of a remarkable residential complex in which wit and lightness of touch are the distinguishing themes.

The 1960s house (which was damaged by fire when Brooks was commissioned) stood in a generous garden in Hampstead, set back from the street behind an enclosing wall. The initial brief was one of repair, conversion and extension, with an extra bedroom and a more generous entrance space to be provided. The project subsequently grew to include a radical reconstruction of the existing house, new structures in the garden and a reconfiguration of the landscape. The architect describes the completed project as "a domestic campus of enclosed, semi-enclosed and open structures". The changes are far from cosmetic and exhibit, for a relatively modest project costing under £600,000, a considerable element of structural bravura by the consultant engineers Price & Myers.

The additional space to the existing house could only be provided on the garden front, where it is conceived as a timber-clad volume hovering over a new glazed terrace and supported on a single 'V' column, painted bright red. Inside, a new suspended staircase, contained within steel mesh, is hung from the first floor within a new central atrium, which is the focus of the house. A free-standing screen wall, the work of artist Simon Patterson, conceals the cloakroom, and a new dining-room has been created where there was formerly an outdoor terrace. New timber decks connect internal and external spaces.

The separate X-pavilion (replacing a double garage and containing a gym and guest accommodation) is conceived as a pure glass box, sitting on a folded *in-situ* concrete plate that provides the base for the building and a retaining wall. Inside, a folded timber plate forms both a floor and a screen wall. The earth-covered roof of the pavilion is carried on two 'X' members.

Finally, the existing car port has been replaced by a new 'O port' – just a roof, dramatically cantilevered, sitting on a light steel structure of which the 'O' forms part. Inside the house, high-quality materials, including aluminium, choice woods, etched glass and limestone, are used freely. The essence of the project seems to be the attempt to erode the barriers between the highly tactile interior and the openness of the garden beyond.

The VXO project – the initials of which are derived from the boldly painted steel structural members – includes the refurbishment of an existing house, the construction of a new glazed pavilion containing gym and guest accommodation, and a new car port. The three buildings form a family of structures within the context of the lushly planted garden.

ARTIGIANO HEADQUARTERS, YARMOUTH, ISLE OF WIGHT
THE MANSER PRACTICE

ARUP CAMPUS, SOLIHULL, WEST MIDLANDS
ARUP ASSOCIATES

BENNETTS ASSOCIATES LONDON OFFICE, ISLINGTON, LONDON EC1
BENNETTS ASSOCIATES

BROADCASTING HOUSE REDEVELOPMENT, BBC, LONDON W1
MacCORMAC JAMIESON PRICHARD

ERCOL FACTORY, PRINCES RISBOROUGH, BUCKINGHAMSHIRE
HORDEN CHERRY LEE ARCHITECTS

27–30 FINSBURY SQUARE, LONDON EC2
ERIC PARRY ARCHITECTS

FORBURY SQUARE, READING, BERKSHIRE
PORPHYRIOS ASSOCIATES/LIFSCHUTZ DAVIDSON

HABERDASHERS' HALL, LONDON EC1
HOPKINS ARCHITECTS

122 LEADENHALL STREET, LONDON EC3
RICHARD ROGERS PARNERSHIP

LYNHER DAIRY CHEESE FACTORY, PONSANOOTH, CORNWALL
SUTHERLAND HUSSEY

MERRILL LYNCH FINANCIAL CENTRE, NEWGATE, LONDON EC1
SWANKE HAYDEN CONNELL ARCHITECTS

THE MINERVA BUILDING, LONDON EC3
NICHOLAS GRIMSHAW & PARTNERS

PACIFIC QUAY, BBC SCOTLAND, GLASGOW
DAVID CHIPPERFIELD ARCHITECTS

ROYEX HOUSE, LONDON WALL, LONDON EC2
ERIC PARRY ARCHITECTS

SWISS RE TOWER, ST MARY AXE, LONDON EC3
FOSTER AND PARTNERS

TOYOTA GB HEADQUARTERS, EPSOM, SURREY
SHEPPARD ROBSON

ARTIGIANO HEADQUARTERS YARMOUTH, ISLE OF WIGHT

THE MANSER PRACTICE, 2001

The Artigiano headquarters are another example of highly pragmatic 'adaptive reuse', motivated less by the desire to retain the existing buildings than by issues of cost and programme. The client, a rapidly expanding mail-order fashion business, had explored the possibility of demolishing the disused farm buildings (a barn and milking shed) on the site to make way for a new headquarters but had failed to gain planning consent. The Manser Practice was commissioned to prepare an alternative conversion scheme with a view to a very fast programme – a maximum four months for construction and fit-out.

The brief demanded accommodation for a mail-order call centre, plus design studios. The two existing sheds were stripped down to their frames and reclad, and the north elevation was glazed floor to ceiling to provide glare-free natural light and views out to the nearby downs. Solid areas of cladding were faced with rough-sawn timber to form a rain screen. The roof is of insulated, profiled steel, largely supported on the existing structure. The materials were chosen for their low cost and ready availability; the construction work was done by a local contractor. New services could easily be accommodated, although ventilation is largely natural, using circulation encouraged by cross-vents. Between the two sheds a fully glazed pavilion contains the main entrance, reception area and management offices, with its southern elevation shaded by a projecting canopy.

The total cost of the project was less than £1,000,000. Although low cost and fast track, the resulting complex has an elegance and a strong image in tune with the business it houses. This could be the future of many agricultural buildings in a Britain where farming is subject to ongoing retraction and rationalization.

ARUP CAMPUS, SOLIHULL, WEST MIDLANDS

ARUP ASSOCIATES, 1999–2001

With the foundation of Arup Associates in 1963 the Arup engineering empire became a multi-disciplinary practice, and under the leadership of Philip Dowson, Peter Foggo and James Burland, Arup Associates has remained a major player on the British architectural scene for four decades. It has always been an innovative practice, not least for its interest in environmental and energy issues; but even in the 1960s it was influenced by the instinctive rationalism of the vernacular tradition.

These themes are reflected in the 'campus' that Arup Associates designed to house up to 400 Arup staff working in a variety of disciplines, from structural engineering to car design. The site, close to the M42 motorway, was chosen for convenience rather than charm. It is part of a routine business park, where the other buildings are typically slick and faceless. Two existing offices, in Coventry and central Birmingham, were merged in the new development, which is Arup's largest office after London and Hong Kong.

The brief demanded a flexible and friendly environment that encouraged interaction between the teams working there. Natural ventilation was also specified, whereas the typical business-park block is air-conditioned. Two pavilions (a third is planned) step down the sloping site and contain four staggered levels of accommodation; a reception area links the two. The steel-framed buildings are clad in untreated timber – which has already weathered to pleasing effect – with louvred shutters, to control solar gain, and opening windows. The distinctive 'chimneys' that punctuate the roofs of the pavilions are dual-purpose, acting as light scoops and extracting stale air (or smoke in the event of a fire). There is an echo here of Snape Maltings concert hall, Suffolk, the pioneering exercise in modern vernacular that Arup Associates designed in the mid-1960s.

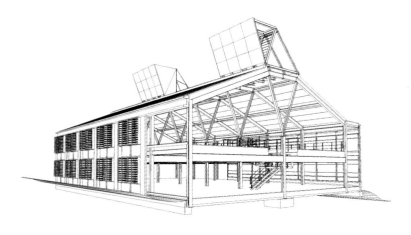

Left and above
The project is based on a low-energy agenda expressed in the 'chimneys' that act both as light scoops and extracts for stale air.

Opposite
The exterior of the buildings is clad in untreated timber, which weathers attractively, and shutters to counteract solar gain.

BENNETTS ASSOCIATES LONDON OFFICE
ISLINGTON, LONDON EC1

BENNETTS ASSOCIATES, 2001–02

The Islington offices of Bennetts Associates, the practice that Rab and Denise Bennetts founded in 1987, have the ambience more of a well-loved studio-cum-home than of a powerhouse of commercial design. Yet it is the growth of the practice, with a solid base of office commissions as well as such public works as the Gateway and Orientation Centre at Loch Lomond (see pp. 104–05), that necessitated the move from its increasingly cramped base just 50 metres (165 feet) down the street.

The complex of buildings in Rawstorne Place, off St John Street, ranging in date from the eighteenth to the mid-twentieth century, was acquired as a result of a clear-out of surplus property by the local authority. It has been converted to house nearly fifty staff. The oldest element was an utterly derelict Georgian barn, once used by drovers taking cattle to Smithfield Market in east London. Historic buildings specialist Richard Griffiths advised on the rescue of this structure, which now houses two conference rooms and the practice library. It has been repaired as found, with rough brickwork and old timbers left exposed. A

new building wraps around the barn hard up against the rear-garden wall of a Victorian terrace; this contains the reception area and open-plan offices, partly in a lightweight mezzanine. It has a planted earth roof (providing excellent insulation) and is lit via a glazed clerestory. A minimal glazed link, containing a staircase, connects the barn to a former printworks, where there are two further floors of design studios, light and airy spaces overlooking the open courtyard.

Bennetts Associates has a reputation for pioneering sustainable design, and everything possible has been done to make this project environmentally responsible. Ventilation is entirely natural, materials found on site have been recycled, even the carpeting is made of recycled PVC. Recycling old buildings is, of course, one of the soundest ways of conserving scarce resources. This intelligent and highly practical mix of old and new provides the practice with an inspirational work space; it should inspire others to seek out the decaying interstices in the fabric of London.

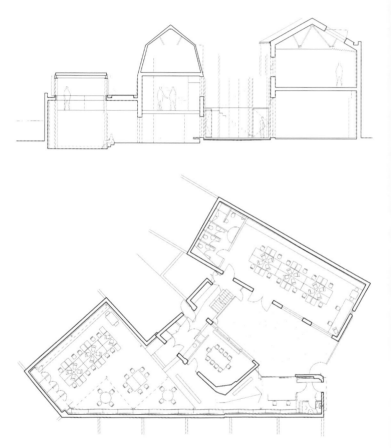

The office complex fills an irregular site that includes buildings that range in date from the eighteenth to the mid-twentieth century. The oldest element is a former barn, a remarkable survival that is now joined to a former printworks by a glazed link building. Around one side of the barn is a new reception area and additional office accommodation.

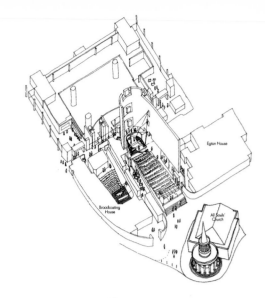

BROADCASTING HOUSE REDEVELOPMENT
BBC, LONDON W1

MacCORMAC JAMIESON PRICHARD, 2000–08

The appointment of MacCormac Jamieson Prichard (MJP) in December 2000 to design a comprehensive reconstruction of the BBC's historic Portland Place site won the practice one of the key London commissions of the early 2000s. Richard MacCormac's scheme, although less explicitly radical than the competing proposal offered by Will Alsop, is about modernizing not only the physical fabric, but also ways of working.

Broadcasting House, designed by Val Myer and opened in 1931, is a classic of the Modernistic manner, little loved by 'progressive' critics of the 1930s but now an established landmark. Plans to extend it were curtailed by the outbreak of war in 1939. The large extensions built during the 1960s, which were unsubtle intrusions into the street scene, with a particularly damaging effect on views from the south of John Nash's church of All Souls, are removed by the redevelopment. Broadcasting House itself is being refurbished and restored.

The MacCormac scheme is part of an ambitious development programme (of which Allies & Morrison's White City project, in west London, is part) that rationalizes the BBC's estate of buildings and sites in London. The 'one BBC' philosophy seeks to break down the divisions between the distinct 'tribes' (as MacCormac sees them) that form the various departments within the organization. All BBC news networks are to be housed at Portland Place, along with BBC Radio and Music. Openness, flexibility and interaction are key themes in the development. The vast newsroom, the largest in the world, is located at lower ground-floor level. A new entrance on the east side of Portland Place leads into the dramatic central route extending across the site, a social space as much as a circulation zone, with restaurants and areas for informal meetings (and the chatter that can generate new programme ideas) close to production areas. There are fine views out to All Souls and Regent Street beyond.

On one level the scheme is highly pragmatic and in line with the criteria of the world of commercial development. At the same time it offers public benefits, not least the new square, adjacent to All Souls, which has been designed as an open-air performance space in fine weather. The architecture takes its cue from the curved form of Myer's building but has a contemporary lightness and ambivalence far removed from the solid Portland stone façades of the 1930s. The etched and printed glass façade that forms the elusive backdrop to Nash's church is a site for architect/artist collaboration; indeed, this is a theme that is being pursued throughout the development. With the Science Museum Wellcome Wing, in South Kensington, and Southwark's Jubilee line station, both in London, this project demonstrates MJP's determination to tackle large-scale urban projects far removed from the intricately crafted university buildings for which it had become known.

The reconstruction of Broadcasting House provides an integrated base for the BBC's news operation, but equally offers enormous gains for the public realm, notably by re-establishing the position of Nash's spire of All Souls, Langham Place, in the townscape.

ERCOL FACTORY, PRINCES RISBOROUGH BUCKINGHAMSHIRE

HORDEN CHERRY LEE ARCHITECTS, 1999–2002

New factories, where physical products are made, are now an uncommon occurrence in a country dependent for its living on financial and other service industries. (Wilkinson Eyre's Dyson factory in Wiltshire was hailed as a harbinger of British industrial revival when it opened in 1998, but Dyson has since transferred much of its manufacturing to the Far East, where labour costs are far cheaper.)

Ercol is a family firm, producing traditional wooden furniture, that has been based in High Wycombe, Buckinghamshire, for eighty years and currently employs 350 people. The new factory was commissioned to replace existing premises in the centre of High Wycombe; the original site has been redeveloped for housing. The new, brownfield site, at Princes Risborough, 11 kilometres (7 miles) away and enclosed by protected woodland, was formerly used by the Building Research Establishment; it has scope for future growth. The new building houses all of Ercol's existing manufacturing and administrative operations, and a showroom for visitors.

The building is, on one level, a restatement of the cool American aesthetic that characterized the best industrial buildings of the 1960s: Roche Dinkeloo's Cummins factory in Indiana, for instance, or Team 4's Reliance Controls factory in Wiltshire. The factory production space is (inevitably) a big economical shed, with grey profiled-metal cladding, but it is set within the 22.5 x 12-metre (74 x 39-foot) grid of the elegant white steel frame, which encloses subsidiary spaces and extends out to embrace the landscape. The visitor experiences the building as a series of layers that mediate between external and internal space; the influence on the diagram of Renzo Piano's Menil Collection, Texas, is acknowledged.

Factories are often claustrophobic places. This one makes maximum use of natural light and offers workers views out: a strip of glazing 120 metres (394 feet) long along one side of the production space gives a prospect of green surroundings, and further daylight is filtered through roof lights. The offices and showroom are also naturally lit, with shading devices to control solar gain; the staff restaurant opening on to the edge of woodland is a particularly attractive space. The environmental and energy credentials of the building appear to be strong: it offers above-average working conditions and has a benign impact on the surrounding area. The project is a quiet but hugely impressive exercise in practical idealism in the best traditions of the Modern Movement, demonstrating that less can still mean more.

Opposite, top, and above
The influence of the work of Mies van der Rohe is seen yet again in the Ercol factory, where a disciplined steel frame contains production and other spaces.

Opposite, bottom
Internally, natural light pervades the production spaces, offices, showroom and staff restaurant.

27–30 FINSBURY SQUARE, LONDON EC2

ERIC PARRY ARCHITECTS, 1999–2002

Eric Parry's redevelopment of nos. 27–30 Finsbury Square (on the edge of the City but just within the borough of Islington) highlights many of the issues underlying the politics of development in the business heart of London.

The site was previously occupied by two buildings, an undistinguished 1960s block deemed obsolete for present-day commercial use, and an inter-war building in a dignified, if commonplace, Classical manner, which was 'locally listed'. Both stood within a conservation area. Finsbury Square, a Georgian development in origin, is now a collection of diverse post-1900 frontages unified only by the prevalence of solid masonry façades: even Foster and Partners' recent building on the corner of Finsbury Pavement bows to this pattern.

Parry's project to redevelop the site was linked to a masterplan (by Latz & Partners) for the reconfiguration of the square, a rather confused space that contains a bowling green, filling station and underground car park. The aim was to make the new building "a wall to a square", a distinctly civic presence. The sophisticated façade to the square, which is of loadbearing stone, engineered with Whitby & Bird, incorporates shading and drainage, and is integrated with the column-free office floors behind.

This is a subtly understated building by an architect whose thoughtful approach is increasingly influencing the London commercial scene. Parry sees the danger of a decreasing area for architecture in a market that demands standardization and economy. "Spaces need weight", he insists. At Finsbury Square he has produced a convincing model for a new masonry-fronted City architecture that is compatible with the spatial demands of the twenty-first-century office.

The façade could be seen as an optional, even a dispensable, feature of the modern office building, but at Finsbury Square Eric Parry has transformed it into a potent civic and public presence.

FORBURY SQUARE, READING, BERKSHIRE

PORPHYRIOS ASSOCIATES/LIFSCHUTZ DAVIDSON, 1999–2003

Demetri Porphyrios is respected beyond 'traditionalist' ranks for his intelligent adaptation of the Classical language of architecture to the demands of the commercial market. Having completed two office buildings at Birmingham's highly successful Brindleyplace quarter, Porphyrios is at work on the masterplan for King's Cross goods yard, a key London development focus of the first decade of the twenty-first century. Working (as at Brindleyplace and King's Cross) for developer Argent, Porphyrios was commissioned to prepare a masterplan for a highly sensitive site close to Forbury Gardens and the medieval church of St Laurence in the centre of Reading – a town badly mauled by crass redevelopment in the 1960s and 1970s. The site had been largely occupied by a drab 1960s office scheme that offered no potential for continued use, with a gap left for the intended inner-relief road (subsequently abandoned).

Porphyrios proposed a mixed-use development, with a twenty-storey residential tower forming one side of a new public square. To the south, the square would be enclosed by an office building, subsequently designed by Lifschutz Davidson. Although endorsed by the

Commission for Architecture and the Built Environment (CABE), the proposals were rejected in 2000 by the local authority: the tower proved predictably contentious. The revised scheme, completed in 2003, provides two office buildings (the residential element was deleted) roughly comparable in height but very different in architectural treatment. Lifschutz Davidson's block (10,200 square metres/110,000 square feet) features a highly glazed envelope enclosing a new pedestrian arcade. Porphyrios's building (4400 square metres/47,300 square feet) is seen as a free-standing pavilion, a formal composition that balances the handsome Shire Hall to the east. The façade to the square is clad in metal and glass; other façades are of brick, with stone dressings. The top storey is a lightweight structure, emphasizing the pavilion idea. Projecting eaves provide a distinctive touch. One is reminded of some of the progressive iron-and-glass commercial buildings of the Victorian era.

Porphyrios's abandoned tower would have been a real landmark, but what has been built is urbane and elegant, with real benefits in terms of public space. Although they are very different in their design philosophy, the two practices appear to have worked together harmoniously.

Porphyrios Associates' office building at Forbury Square in Reading combines solid load-bearing masonry with lightweight glazing, used in the manner of Victorian commercial and industrial buildings.

HABERDASHERS' HALL, LONDON EC1

HOPKINS ARCHITECTS, 1996–2002

Below
The hall is housed in a collegiate-style quadrangle behind Smithfield. The palette of materials – load-bearing brick with a lead roof – is typical of Hopkins.

Opposite
Hopkins' reinterpretation of a great hall, with its diagrid roof and timber panelling, has a lightness that depends on the use of modern structural technology.

To outsiders, the culture of City livery companies is a mystery. Are these institutions little more than élitist dining clubs, a variant of freemasonry irrelevant to modern business? The fact that the Haberdashers' Company (first given a royal charter in 1448) supports eight schools, with over 6000 pupils, suggests that there is a little more to it than that (although haberdashers do not figure prominently in the commercial life of modern London).

The first Haberdashers' Hall burned in the Great Fire of London (1666); the second was destroyed by bombs in the Second World War. In recent years the company, with over 800 members, was housed in an undistinguished 1950s building by the obscure A.S. Ash, which was sold for redevelopment in the mid-1990s when the Haberdashers acquired a site at West

Smithfield for their new hall. The site has been redeveloped with a new office building (a serviceable Hopkins design) along Hosier Lane and sixty-five apartments plus shops developed by British Land in a converted Edwardian block. The hall itself is housed in a central quadrangle at the secluded heart of the site.

The Haberdashers might seem a tailor-made Hopkins client. In recent years the Hopkins office has been adept at designing for old British institutions – public schools and colleges; Lord's Cricket Ground, in London; Goodwood racecourse, West Sussex; Glyndebourne opera house, East Sussex; even the House of Commons, in London. This is the world inhabited by City liverymen. As before, Hopkins has responded with a modern architecture rooted in history and finding expression in

traditional materials; you would not expect a City company to commission Zaha Hadid or David Adjaye.

The starting-point of the project is the skiful strategy for the development of the site. In most circumstances, the landlocked central plot would be the hardest to develop, but it is the ideal location for the two-storey collegiate-style hall, entered via an arch off West Smithfield. The formal rooms – main dining-hall and other social spaces, court and committee rooms, and library – are on the first floor. Below are offices, cloakrooms, kitchens and other ancillary spaces arranged around a cloistered green quadrangle; on the north side the open cloister arcade is glazed in to form an orangery. There is a clear processional route from point of entry to dining-table.

The overall look of the building recalls Glyndebourne (and, for that matter, the residential block that Hopkins added to the Charterhouse, on the far side of Smithfield): loadbearing brick walls, finely detailed precast concrete left exposed, lead-covered roofs and high-quality timberwork. The approach embodies "a balance between change and tradition", say the architects. The livery hall is clearly the climax of the building. Its diagrid timber roof and oak panelling produce a rich and intimate atmosphere, modern but acceptable to the most entrenched traditionalist. This is well-crafted architecture with integrity and appropriateness, although it revisits familiar themes in the practice's work of the 1990s. The future direction of Hopkins's architecture is a matter of considerable interest.

122 LEADENHALL STREET, LONDON EC3

RICHARD ROGERS PARTNERSHIP, 2002–

Rogers's Leadenhall Street tower is a striking addition to a cluster of towers that includes Foster's Swiss Re and includes a generous public space at street level.

Having completed the City's only post-war building of international significance – Lloyd's of London (1986) – Richard Rogers Parnership returned to the Square Mile in the 1990s with 88 Wood Street and Lloyd's Register of Shipping, both major works by the practice. The forty-seven-storey, 80,000-square-metre (850,000-square-foot) tower on Leadenhall Street, replacing a 1960s block opposite Lloyd's, forms part of a cluster of towers, including Norman Foster's Swiss Re tower (see p. 219), in this sector of the City.

The tapering form of the tower, with its distinctive bracing, reflects the structural diagram of a vertical cantilever and recalls the John Hancock building in Chicago by Skidmore, Owings & Merrill (SOM). Floors of varying sizes provide flexible spaces suitable either for open-plan or cellular offices, and respond to the varied demands of City organizations.

Unlike many towers, the building does not use the traditional principle of a central core to achieve structural stability, but instead employs a full-perimeter braced tube, using the extremities of the floorplate to create stability under wind loads at high levels. This principle allows the core elements to be expressed externally in 'servant' towers on the north side of the building, giving legibility to the overall composition. The occupied floorspace (the 'served' areas) are therefore preserved as open and flexible, with minimal internal structure.

The lower levels of the tower are cut away to form a covered public space and an extension of the adjacent piazza, which is animated by cafés, restaurants and shops.

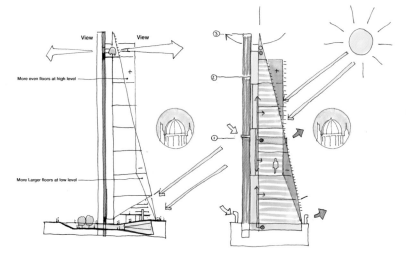

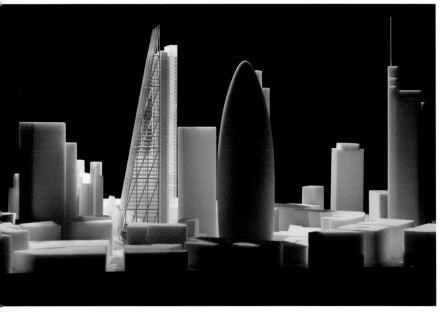

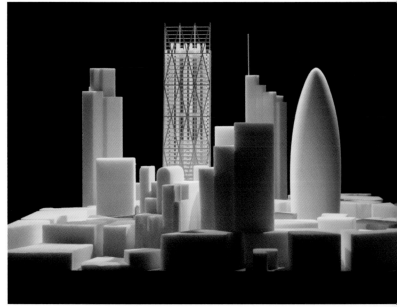

Extremely straightforward and extremely utilitarian, this factory servicing a growing local industry is a symbol of the potential renewal of rural England.

LYNHER DAIRY CHEESE FACTORY
PONSANOOTH, CORNWALL
SUTHERLAND HUSSEY, 2001–02

This was Edinburgh-based Sutherland Hussey's first completed building, and, modest though it is, it makes you want to see the company work on a larger scale.

The project started on site in the middle of the 2001 outbreak of foot-and-mouth disease, which posed considerable problems for architects and contractors. The client was a local farmer (the brother-in-law of one of the architects), heeding the call for agriculture to diversify by manufacturing Yarg cheese, an increasingly popular regional delicacy. The success of the business meant that a new production building was needed – and quickly. An off-the-peg portal frame shed might have fitted the bill, but the new building was not strictly for agricultural use and planning consent

was needed. A relatively discreet approach was demanded by planners.

The form of the building is very simple, accommodating sealed production and storage areas plus an office and a small communal area for staff. A hygienic shed was all that was necessary. But there are sheds – and sheds. The fact that this is a traditional post-and-beam structure is clearly expressed, with the fibrous cement roof overhanging the building like a canopy. Cladding is of plain Douglas fir boarding. It is all very straightforward but in rural England the choice these days is generally between the pretentious and the lumberingly utilitarian, which is why this building merits attention.

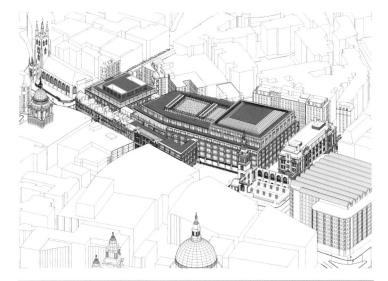

MERRILL LYNCH FINANCIAL CENTRE
NEWGATE, LONDON EC1

SWANKE HAYDEN CONNELL ARCHITECTS, 1996–2001

The Merrill Lynch development at Newgate, close to St Paul's Cathedral, is – at 80,000 square metres (860,000 square feet) – one of London's largest office schemes. It is remarkable, however, not only for its scale, but also for its positive impact on the public realm and imaginative approach to the reuse of historic buildings. Swanke Hayden Connell Architects (SHCA), like Merrill Lynch a firm with American roots, was brought in soon after a business merger, gathering various arms of the company under one roof, made the construction of new premises a priority. None of the buildings on offer, either completed or planned, was suitable for Merrill Lynch's requirements, which included space for very large dealing floors. The company therefore acquired the site at Newgate, largely occupied by a redundant postal sorting office, which until the 1900s had been the site of the public school Christ's Hospital and, before the Reformation in the sixteenth century, of the London house of the Franciscan order. On the eastern edge of the site stands the remains of Sir Christopher Wren's Christ Church, gutted by wartime bombs and partly demolished as late as the 1970s for road widening – an appalling act of vandalism. The southern edge of the site is enclosed by a run of Victorian buildings, which the City had long planned to raze for yet more road surface but had effectively conceded would have to be retained and refurbished.

Under the Merrill Lynch scheme the former sorting office, a listed building, was demolished with the approval of English Heritage, which agreed that it had no potential for reuse. A very large block housing two trading floors, each of more than 6000 square metres (65,000 square feet), now occupies the centre of the site. Another new block addresses Giltspur Street to the west. To the east, the former post office has been refurbished as a conference and exhibition space. The architecture of the new buildings is dignified, solid and unfussy, with brick and stone cladding framing large window openings, an approach that contrasts with the blatant façadism of much Post-modernist work of the 1980s. An impressive glazed galleria connects the dealing-floor block with retained buildings on Newgate Street.

The chief success of the scheme, however, lies in its expansion and improvement of the public routes and spaces within the site. A generous cloister frames the former churchyard of Christ Church, which has been landscaped as an attractive garden, with its lost railings reinstated. A further public route extends from Newgate Street behind the restored Victorian buildings; the ground floors are let as shops and cafés. The scheme shows how large modern financial operations can be accommodated, quite painlessly, at the heart of the City. The pity is that there is probably no other comparable site available in the Square Mile – hence the ongoing push into Spitalfields and Shoreditch.

The Merrill Lynch project combines the use of existing buildings with state-of-the-art offices for a major financial institution, and focuses internally on a glazed galleria, part of a public route through the site.

THE MINERVA BUILDING, LONDON EC3
NICHOLAS GRIMSHAW & PARTNERS, 1999–

The Minerva Building is conceived as a series
of intersecting planes breaking down the mass
of the structure and responding to its urban
context. The building would be an elegant addition
to the eastern quarter of the City.

Grimshaw's Minerva tower (designed for
client Minerva plc) is one of the most
promising of the various proposals for tall
buildings in and around the City of London
that emerged in the first years of the twenty-
first century. The present (2002) scheme is
Grimshaw's second for the Aldgate site; its
predecessor, commissioned in 1999, a tower
of rather squat proportions notable for the
scale of the floorplates it offered, was
abandoned after receiving a notably cool
reception from City planners and the
Commission for Architecture and the Built
Environment (CABE). It is interesting to note
that Minerva's existing planning consent,
granted in 1999, provided for a fourteen-
storey block with 46,500 square metres
(500,000 square feet) of office space,
whereas Grimshaw's building will be 217
metres (712 feet) tall with 93,000 square
metres (1,000,000 square feet) of lettable
space – the largest free-standing office
building in the City.

The City-fringe site, at the junction of
Houndsditch and St Botolph Street, was
historically a gateway to the Square Mile, a
fact that underlines the case for a landmark
structure there. The 1980s office boom
extended to Aldgate: one of the most
prominent neighbours is the direly Post-
modernist Beaufort House of 1986–88.
Objections to the Minerva tower have
focused both on its impact on the City
skyline and on its relationship to the
Georgian church of St Botolph, yet this could
be an exciting juxtaposition, just as I.M. Pei's
crystalline Hancock Tower provides a striking

backdrop to Trinity Church in Boston,
Massachusetts. At present, the church is
marooned on a traffic island, so the Minerva
scheme could be the catalyst for a radical
reconfiguration of the surrounding area.
Existing buildings to be demolished include
an ugly multi-storey car park.

The elegant (but quite complex) form of
the building reflects its operational agenda:
it could be a wholly occupied headquarters
or easily be subdivided, in line with the
demands of the market. The architects see it
as a series of open books of varying height,
the asymmetry of the plan, with four façade
planes dividing the site diagonally,
responding to the context of streets and
routes. The theme of asymmetry extends
into the section of the building. The repetitive
floor pattern of the past is jettisoned in
favour of a sophisticated mix of spaces. The
sky lobby, halfway up the tower, is the social
heart of the building, accessed directly by
double-decker express lifts. The ground floor
contains 2000 square metres (22,000 square
feet) of retailing served by new pedestrian
arcades. The rooftop restaurant has its own
dedicated lift service.

Grimshaw's concern for detail is famous
and there is no doubt that this will be a finely
crafted building. As is now customary, the
developer argues that it would also be
'sustainable', a claim always hard to
quantify. Double-skin façades, with opening
windows on the inner skin, and an element
of natural ventilation – although conventional
air-conditioning is also provided – could,
however, significantly reduce energy usage.

PACIFIC QUAY, BBC SCOTLAND, GLASGOW
DAVID CHIPPERFIELD ARCHITECTS, 2001–04

David Chipperfield's victory in the 2001 competition for the BBC's new headquarters at Pacific Quay, Glasgow, was something of a landmark. Chipperfield has won major commissions in the Far East, the USA and throughout Europe, including new law courts in Barcelona, the reconstruction of Berlin's Neues Museum and an extension to Venice's cemetery island of San Michele. Yet his only completed schemes in Britain are on a small scale. Pacific Quay looks set to be a significant work, reflecting Chipperfield's legendary skills in the manipulation of space and light and passionate interest in materials. The project is part of a concerted building campaign by the BBC, which includes Richard MacCormac's radical recasting and expansion of Broadcasting House (see pp. 202–03) and Allies & Morrison's redevelopment of the White City site in London, as well as major building campaigns in regional centres.

The site is on the banks of the River Clyde, in an area of ongoing regeneration across the river from Norman Foster's 'armadillo' convention centre. It was used for a garden festival in the 1980s and Building Design Partnership's Glasgow Science Centre (see pp. 60–61) is another of its new attractions. The brief called for a mix of studio spaces and offices in a building that would be accessible to the public and encourage creative interaction among staff.

The key feature of the competition-winning scheme is the internal landscape in which a stepped terrace, clad in stone and covering the various studio spaces (which do not require daylight), provides the social heart of the building, along with a great variety of scenarios for informal meetings. The offices look down into the naturally lit central atrium. Externally, the aim was to make the building as transparent as possible, although the treatment of the façades has since been significantly rethought.

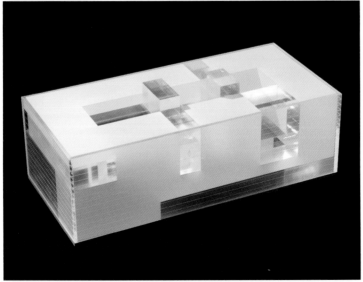

Opposite
BBC Scotland headquarters forms one element in the regeneration campaign for the former industrial land on the banks of the Clyde.

Left
Within the simple rectangular building the interior consists of a landscape of social and circulation space around the enclosed studios, with offices overlooking a central atrium.

ROYEX HOUSE, LONDON WALL, LONDON EC2
ERIC PARRY ARCHITECTS, 2001–

At Finsbury Square, a short distance from London Wall, Eric Parry recently completed a building (see p. 206) that is essentially about context, in particular about relating to the square itself, with its formal Georgian origins. His proposal for the redevelopment of Royex House, a run-of-the-mill block by Richard Seifert at the junction of London Wall and Wood Street, has a very different agenda. "It's an iconic, not a street, building", he says. The area has undergone extensive redevelopment over the last twenty years. Across London Wall is Terry Farrell's massive Alban Gate, forming a new portal to the Barbican. Wood Street has recent buildings by Norman Foster and Richard Rogers as well as McMorran & Whitby's police station, a quirky Classical exercise, and the surviving tower of St Alban's Church by Sir Christopher Wren. Guildhall is just a stone's throw away.

The challenge at Royex House was that of providing larger floorplates and a substantial increase in usable space on a constricted site, while offering major improvements to the public realm – to which the Seifert block, designed in conjunction with the now discredited upper-level walkway route, offered nothing. The new building is eighteen storeys high, with accommodation in two staggered wings, linked by a triple-height lobby area, but the subtlety of its gently tapering form, combined with the façade treatment, reduces its perceived impact on the skyline. The lobby area is public space, creating a new link between Wood Street and Aldermanbury Square. Existing high-level walkways are to be demolished.

Royex House has column-free floors with structure around the edges. The façade is of textured stainless steel, arranged in double-height panels – a further device to reduce the apparent height and bulk of the building.

The form of Royex House responds both to the ordered townscape of Wood Street and to the larger scale of London Wall, and creates a new public space at street level.

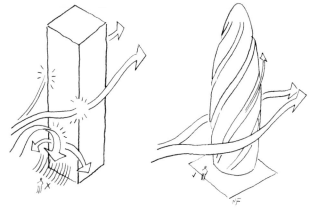

SWISS RE TOWER, ST MARY AXE, LONDON EC3

FOSTER AND PARTNERS, 1997–2004

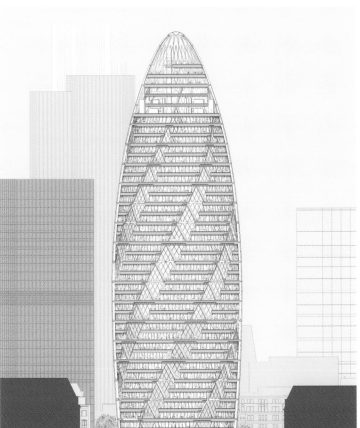

The Swiss Re tower stands on the site of the Baltic Exchange, an elaborate but essentially undistinguished Edwardian pile irreparably wrecked by a terrorist bomb in 1992 and subsequently cleared away. Its neighbours include the medieval church of St Helen, Bishopsgate (itself damaged in the same outrage), Gollins Melvin Ward Partnership's 1960s Commercial Union tower (another victim of the bomb, since conscientiously restored) and Richard Rogers's Lloyd's of London – a typically variegated City mix. Even before its completion, Swiss Re has become a familiar and largely popular London landmark. Designed by a team led by Norman Foster's partner Ken Shuttleworth, and with a strong input from Foster himself, the forty-storey building (40,000 square metres/430,000 square feet) is very much a bespoke project, developing the innovative themes seen nearly thirty years ago in Foster's superb Willis Faber & Dumas headquarters, Ipswich, and more recently in the Frankfurt Commerzbank. It makes an interesting comparison with the more conventional office projects across the City designed by the same practice, for example on London Wall, in Finsbury Square, at Tower Gateway and, across the river in Southwark, in the More London development that forms an extension of London Bridge City.

The tower (ludicrously nicknamed 'the erotic gherkin') will house Swiss Re's London headquarters, although a proportion of it is now being let to tenants. One of Foster's strengths lies in his ability to persuade hard-headed clients to run with radical ideas, but it is doubtful if British Land or Stanhope would have built anything quite as remarkable as this. The nature of the project limits the scope for the standardization beloved of the development industry. (Ironically, Foster's City Hall was built to a more rigorous developer brief – and it shows.) Circular floors are generally seen as difficult to let and to use, but Foster addresses this issue by dividing the floors into basically rectangular fingers, separated by triangular voids that maximize natural light and the flow of fresh air via the double-skin façade. The staggered form of the floorplates as they rise up the tower allows daylight to penetrate deep into the building. A series of sky gardens (or 'bio-climatic terraces'), somewhat reduced in the final version of the scheme, are both part of the low-energy environmental strategy and have a function as social/interactive spaces. Retailing and restaurants occupy the lower floors of the tower, serving a new public square around the base. The form of the building has been designed with aerodynamic performance in mind, and the square, it is claimed, will be free of the gusts that so many tall buildings generate.

Swiss Re is, by any standards, a memorable building and a symbol of the continuing vitality of the City. It reflects Foster's continuing quest for innovation and his response to the vogue for strong form in architecture. Yet the roots of the project can be seen in the work of Buckminster Fuller, the visionary designer who was the single greatest influence on the development of Norman Foster's work.

The Swiss Re tower is already an iconic, memorable and internationally known addition to the London skyline.

TOYOTA GB HEADQUARTERS EPSOM, SURREY

SHEPPARD ROBSON, 1997–2001

The Toyota headquarters in Epsom, along with the Motorola factory at Swindon and the 'Helix' building at Finsbury Pavement in the City of London, is a symbol of long-established Sheppard Robson's rebirth as one of the sharpest and most style-conscious British commercial practices of the twenty-first century. As the even more recent, award-winning scheme for Pfizer at Tadworth, Surrey, confirms, Sheppard Robson can now compete convincingly with practices such as Foster and Partners and Richard Rogers Partnership for jobs of this kind. Its dramatic, even overstated version of High-tech appeals to the world of international business; it could not be more appropriate for the automobile industry, which thrives on futuristic fantasy.

The commission was won in a 1997 competition. The site had previously housed a pharmaceutical research facility, an ugly sprawl of mostly mundane structures around a listed Georgian house but surrounded by remnants of mature parkland. The client wanted a high-profile building, in tune with the Toyota brand, which offered outstanding facilities for 500 staff and the opportunity for new ways of working in an 'open-work culture'.

The 14,000-square-metre (150,000-square-foot) building is designed to take advantage of its restored parkland setting, enhanced by the creation of a new lake. Its diagram provides four two-storey fingers of relatively straightforward office accommodation (a mix of open-plan and cellular) fanning out from a dramatic glazed 'street' 80 metres (260 feet) long containing all circulation and service cores, meeting spaces and support facilities. Much of the really creative work is done in this interactive space. The building is entered via a three-storey rotunda, a showcase structure designed to impress visitors – cars are suspended from the ceiling – that contains a conference suite and staff facilities, including a restaurant and a fitness centre.

Constructed on an *in-situ* concrete frame, the building uses the thermal mass of exposed precast concrete floors as part of an energy-saving servicing strategy. Air-conditioning was stipulated but a sophisticated Arup-engineered double-skin façade, with extensive sun shading, greatly reduces solar load while allowing a high degree of transparency; opening windows in the office areas cuts down energy use in warm weather. The predominant aesthetic is, however, one of glazing and smooth aluminium cladding, in tune with Toyota's product. The architects warmed to this association, as the occasional allusion to car design testifies, such as ducts resembling twin exhausts. This is a slick, international-quality building for a global business, a symbol of the aspirations of post-industrial Britain.

Slick and finely engineered, the Toyota headquarters building reflects the image of the international company for which it was designed. Externally and internally, it is as much a sophisticated advertisement for Toyota as a functional working environment.

BALTIC RESTAURANT, SOUTHWARK, LONDON SE1

SETH STEIN ARCHITECTS/DRURY BROWNE ARCHITECTS
2001–02

The Baltic Restaurant is a conversion of a nineteenth-century carriage works. The spatial drama of the project derives from the contrast between the generously lit restaurant and the more intimate and even mysterious bar area.

Located across the street from Richard MacCormac's Southwark station (part of the Jubilee line extension), the Baltic Restaurant is one of many new businesses that have opened in Southwark in the wake of Tate Modern. It is the work of one of London's most accomplished 'interior architects', Seth Stein, much of whose work has been outside Britain since he left the office of Richard Rogers. The project was executed in association with Drury Browne Architects.

The Baltic utilizes the long-abandoned premises of a former coach-building firm,

tacked on to the rear of a Georgian terrace on Blackfriars Road. Creating an entrance from the street meant enticing customers through a relatively cramped space as a prelude to the main volume of the restaurant, lofty and daylit, which is located in the former coach works. The spatial drama of the interior derives from the contrast between this space and the low, corridor-like bar, dimly lit and with a lacquered steel bar extending along one side.

Seth Stein's strong feeling for textures and materials is well reflected in this

project. Wherever possible original features have been retained, such as the roof trusses in the restaurant. Floors are of bare, black concrete, and the brickwork has been left exposed. Baltic amber, enclosed in translucent panels or suspended on fibre, is used as a feature in the bar. The effect is refined and far from extravagant, generating the ethos of comfort and sophisticated glamour with apparently simple moves.

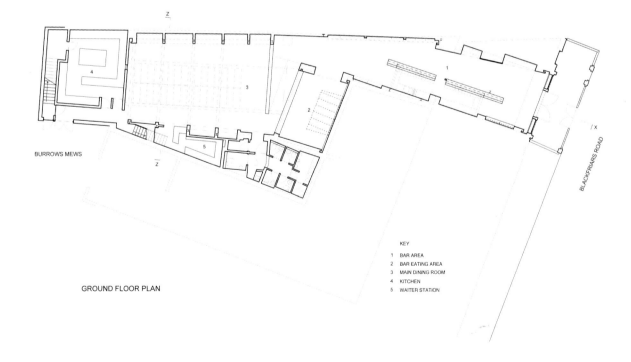

BURROWS MEWS

BLACKFRIARS ROAD

KEY

1 BAR AREA
2 BAR EATING AREA
3 MAIN DINING ROOM
4 KITCHEN
5 WAITER STATION

GROUND FLOOR PLAN

THE RESTAURANT, MANCHESTER

STEPHENSON BELL, 2000–01

The name of this establishment sounds presumptuous but The Restaurant was, for a time at least, *the* fashionable Manchester eatery. Stephenson Bell has a reputation for resuscitating old buildings: Smithfield Buildings in Manchester, completed for developers Urban Splash in 1998, remains one of the outstanding mixed-use city-centre regeneration schemes in any British city. At The Restaurant, the raw material was not a derelict nineteenth-century structure but a 1960s office and retail block, a decent but unexceptional design by Leach, Rhodes & Walker on John Dalton Street, at the very heart of Manchester. The ground floor was for some years the Manchester branch of home-furnishing store Habitat – one of the first in the provinces.

The conversion included the first floor, which had previously been offices with no direct link to the ground floor. The kitchen and formal restaurant are on this level, with a more informal brasserie and bar below. Getting customers to climb stairs is one of the challenges of the restaurant trade. Stephenson Bell entices them with a remarkable staircase, formed of timber treads on stainless-steel cables. The best tables are located in a new glazed pavilion, sitting on a 1960s podium, looking over the street; this lightweight structure, framelessly glazed and with a projecting copper-clad roof, contrasts with the heavy concrete panels of the 1960s block. This contrast continues with the glass canopy that extends into the street and along the entire length of the ground-floor bar. The palette of materials used inside the restaurant – the travertine was inspired by a visit to Harry's Bar in Venice – reflects an emphasis on comfort rather than purity, although the 1960s structure emerges at various points to remind diners of the history of the place.

A new glazed pavilion has been constructed on an existing 1960s podium, and is accessed by a steel-and-timber staircase that is a *tour de force* in terms of its structural ingenuity.

Selfridges, Birmingham, an extraordinary scultural object clad in spun aluminium disks, is a key ingredient in the city's largely post-war city centre. The building is accessed on a number of levels, and a glazed bridge connects to car parking.

The new Selfridges in Birmingham is the largest built work to date of one of the most creative and inspirational figures on the British architectural scene: Jan Kaplicky. With partner Amanda Levete, Czech-born Kaplicky, resident in Britain since 1968, has transformed Future Systems from a visionary studio – in Britain, "visionary" tends to mean impractical – to a practice that is making its mark on city and country.

The project was generated, first, by the ongoing reconstruction of Birmingham's commercial core, intended to remedy the mistakes of the 1960s, tame the traffic and create people-friendly spaces. It was Vittorio Radice, however, the chief executive who recast Selfridges during the 1990s as a style leader, who made the decision to commission Future Systems for

the company's new Birmingham store and to give it a distinct identity in the context of Benoy's huge (and commonplace) £800,000,000 Bullring development (which replaces a failed shopping centre of the 1960s). The retained Rotunda tower and the intricate mass of St Martin's Church, Victorian but standing on an ancient site, are the only "historic" artefacts in the immediate vicinity.

The highly sculptural external form of the store is memorable in the way that Jørn Utzon's Sydney Opera House, Frank Gehry's Guggenheim Bilbao and Nicholas Grimshaw's Eden Project in Cornwall are memorable. These are cultural buildings, however, and Selfridges is about selling fashionable goods – everything from designer frocks to sushi. The impact of Selfridges on

central Birmingham is comparable to that made by the new Peter Jones store on the King's Road in Chelsea, in pre-war London. About 2400 square metres (25,000 square feet) of retail space is provided on four levels. At 4.5 metres (15 feet) high, the spaces are loftier than those of the typical department store. The lowest level contains a food hall fitted out by Future Systems; David Adjaye, Eldridge Smerin and Stanton Williams have been responsible for other internal elements. The interior is illuminated by a dramatic full-height atrium that filters daylight into the retail spaces and is crossed by escalators. A restaurant is planned around the rooftop garden.

The store can be entered at four points: a striking bridge, designed by Future Systems and suspended from the main

structure of the building, connects to car parking and public-transport facilities. Externally, the building has windows only at street level: large, irregular masses of glazing intended to catch the eye of passing drivers as well as pedestrians. The entire structure is an eye-catcher, however, with its cladding formed from approximately 15,000 spun aluminium disks, each about 600 millimetres (24 inches) across. With these enlarged versions of the sequins adorning a stylish dress, sparkling by day and night, the store hardly needs signage.

Selfridges is reportedly planning new stores in other British cities, with some interesting names mentioned as potential architects. Whether the bravura of the Radice era can be rekindled remains to be seen.

SELFRIDGES, MANCHESTER

ADJAYE ASSOCIATES/BUILDING DESIGN PARTNERSHIP/
CIBIC & PARTNERS/FUTURE SYSTEMS/STANTON
WILLIAMS/VINCENT VAN DUYSEN, 2001–02

The reconstruction of Manchester's retail heart that took place after the terrorist bombing of June 1996 was nothing if not ambitious. Marks & Spencer's new store, designed by Building Design Partnership (BDP) and opened in 1999, was the largest M&S anywhere. Too large, it seems, since half of the building has since been sold to Selfridges and fitted out as a high-fashion luxury store with design as a key element in its marketing strategy. The project was in line with the ambitious development plans of Selfridges' former chief executive, Vittorio Radice, responsible for a radical makeover of the Oxford Street store, London, and the commissioning of a new store by Future Systems in Birmingham (see pp. 228–29).

The adaptation of the building was managed by Stanton Williams, with a reconfigured entrance from Exchange Square, new internal connections and a spacious central arcade (designed with BDP). Stanton Williams was also responsible for the second-floor fashion department and restaurant: cool, rational and minimal in the manner that the practice has made its own.

The contributions of David Adjaye and Future Systems are more individual and form the elements that make this store special. Adjaye was given the key ground-floor area, where expensive beauty products and fashionable accessories by big-name designers are displayed. Mirrors and glass are used to create a glamorous but rigorous aesthetic, which is not that of the conventional department store. Even more striking is Future Systems' basement food hall, a taster for the new Birmingham store. While Adjaye works with the grid of the building, Kaplicky and Levete subvert it, with curving walls, randomly placed lighting and lightweight, moveable display units that allow views across the space. A visit is recommended to capture the essence of 'Vogue'-friendly chic in the early 2000s. Who knows how soon the first revamping will begin?

The range of interiors within the store offers a variety of visual experiences for the shopper and reflects the involvement of a number of architectural practices in its fit-out.

TESCO SUPERMARKET, LUDLOW, SHROPSHIRE

MacCORMAC JAMIESON PRICHARD, 1996–2001

For Ludlow, the Tesco supermarket chain abandoned its usual architectural approach for a refined version of the shed, which pays some regard to the context of a historic town.

Ludlow, close to the Welsh border, is one of England's choicest historic towns. Still dominated by its famous castle and magnificent parish church, packed with listed buildings and unspoiled by recent development, it functions well as a prosperous commercial centre for the surrounding rural area. The very idea of a supermarket being built in Ludlow was controversial from the start. Such a development, it was argued, would damage small businesses and form an unacceptable intrusion into the cherished scene, generating increased traffic.

The closure in the 1980s of Ludlow's cattle market, which lay to the north of the town near the railway station, provided a site that, it was argued, was ideal for a supermarket, since it was removed from the historic core but still in walking distance of the town centre. Changes in government policy, discouraging out-of-town retail developments, bolstered the case. Two planning inquiries (in 1994 and 1996) were, however, needed to establish the principle of developing the site; even then, all the designs offered were rejected as unworthy of the town. After the 1996 inquiry, MacCormac Jamieson Prichard (MJP) was brought in to rethink the scheme completely. Tesco, the potential developer,

had become identified with a style in which fake historical details, such as half-timbering, pediments, fancy brickwork and clock towers, were used to disguise the essential element in any supermarket: a large shed containing the merchandise and the check-outs. Such an exercise would have been an insult to a genuinely historic town of this quality.

MJP's achievement was to accept the inevitability of the shed, to decline to disguise or hide it and instead to make it something elegant and distinctive – and unashamedly modern. The roof of the Ludlow store is a shallow 'S', cantilevered out on the car park side to form a *porte-cochère*. Seen from a distance, it sits comfortably into the contours of the town, although the car park (and the traffic it generates) remains an inescapable intrusion. On Corve Street, the character of which is defined by modest eighteenth- and nineteenth-century buildings, the brick façade that encircles the development emerges as a two-storey block, recognizably related to the historic townscape. The fit-out of the store is the standard Tesco product, but the airy grace of MacCormac's shed remains uncompromised. Whether Ludlow needed a supermarket is an issue that continues to be debated.

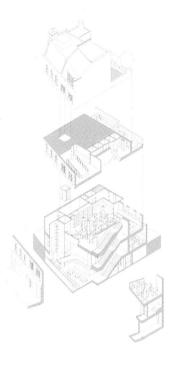

WEST STREET BAR AND RESTAURANT
COVENT GARDEN, LONDON WC2
WELLS MACKERETH ARCHITECTS, 2000–01

London cannot claim a single classic modern restaurant interior of any vintage and it is anyone's guess how long the creations of recent years (by such architects as Rick Mather, Lifschutz Davidson and Seth Stein) will last. West Street, located on the edge of Covent Garden, is an ambitious attempt to combine a fashionable restaurant and bar with a three-room designer hotel.

The setting is a pair of existing, quite unremarkable, buildings dating from around 1900. These have been radically reconstructed; externally the most obvious change is the new barrel-vaulted roof, beneath which is located the best of the guest rooms. The restaurant occupies the ground- and first-floor spaces (the ground floor is an informal brasserie), with the bar in the basement. A full-height window to the street acts as an enticement and advertisement: the bar can be looked into through a void (which extends upwards to the first floor), with a bridge leading into the restaurant. A private dining-room and offices fill the second floor.

The quality of West Street lies not only in dynamic spatial effects, but also in the care and thoroughness of the fit-out, with the architects very much in charge. Furnishings are of particularly high quality, matched by sensuous finishes in stone, metal and wood. The decision to commission signage from master designer Alan Fletcher typifies the thoroughgoing commitment of the client to quality. Fashions may change, and West Street may be a victim, but this is a place of real character, a worthy successor to such historic Covent Garden establishments as Rules and The Ivy.

The West Street interior is remarkable both for its spatial qualities and the very high quality of its furnishings and finishes. The development includes a designer hotel as well as a bar and restaurant.

FURTHER READING

Architecture Foundation, The, *New Architects 2: A Guide to Britain's Best Young Architectural Practices*, London (Merrell) 2001

Borden, Ian, *Manual: The Architecture and Offices of Allford Hall Monaghan Morris*, Basel (Birkhauser) 2003

Davies, Colin, *Hopkins 2*, London (Phaidon) 2001

Farrell, Terry, *Ten Years, Ten Cities: The Work of Terry Farrell and Partners, 1991–2001*, London (Laurence King) 2002

Foster and Partners, *Foster Catalogue 2001*, Munich (Prestel) 2001

Hands, David, and Parker, Sarah, *Manchester: A Guide to Recent Architecture*, London (Ellipsis) 2000

Hardingham, Samantha, *London: A Guide to Recent Architecture*, 5th edn, London (Ellipsis) 2002

Jenkins, David, *On Foster … Foster On*, Munich (Prestel) 2000

Jenkins, David (ed.), *Norman Foster, Works 1*, Munich (Prestel) 2003

John, Richard, and Watkin, David, *John Simpson: The Queen's Gallery, Buckingham Palace, and Other Works*, London (Andreas Papadakis) 2002

Latham, Ian, and Swenarton, Mark, *Jeremy Dixon & Edward Jones: Buildings and Projects, 1959–2002*, London (Right Angle) 2002

LeCruyer, Annette (ed.), *Allies and Morrison: Michigan Architecture Papers, Two*, Ann Arbor (University of Michigan) 1996

Ockman, Joan, and Muller, Lars, *Rafael Viñoly*, Basel (Birkhauser) 2002

Porphyrios Associates: Recent Work, London (Andreas Papadakis) 1999

Powell, Kenneth, *Culture of Building: The Architecture of John McAslan & Partners*, London (Merrell) 2004

Powell, Kenneth, *KPF Europe: Vision and Process*, Basel (Birkhauser) 2003

Powell, Kenneth, *New London Architecture*, London (Merrell) 2001

Powell, Kenneth, *Richard Rogers, Complete Works II*, London (Phaidon) 2001

Powell, Kenneth, *Stephenson Bell Projects*, London (RIBA Publications) 2001

Powell, Kenneth, *Will Alsop 1990–2000*, London (Laurence King) 2002

Richard Murphy Architects: Ten Years of Practice, Edinburgh (Fruitmarket Gallery) 2001

Rodger, Johnny, *Edinburgh: A Guide to Recent Architecture*, London (Ellipsis) 2002

Wilkinson, Chris, and Eyre, James, *Bridging Art and Science: Wilkinson Eyre Architecture*, London (Booth-Clibborn Editions) 2001